SMALL COMPANIES, BIG WINNERS

SMALL COMPANIES, BIG WINNERS

Making Small Companies Really *Work*

Les Green

The Book Guild Ltd
Sussex, England

First published in Great Britain in 2001 by
The Book Guild Ltd
25 High Street
Lewes, East Sussex
BN7 2LU

Typesetting in Times by
Acorn Bookwork, Salisbury, Wiltshire

Printed in Great Britain by
Bookcraft (Bath) Ltd, Avon

A catalogue record for this book is available from
The British Library.

ISBN 1 85776 529 X

Contents

CONTENTS

1 Introduction

This aim of this book is to help anyone who might be considering, is in the process of starting or has recently formed their own small company. It considers: the rules constituting business in general; issues concerning financing and cash flow; sales and marketing practices; internal processes and systems; and the eventual exit and valuation of the company.

The book is targeted at the entrepreneurial small business unit – anything from a sole trader to a private limited company employing less than, say, 50 staff and/or with annual sales revenues of not more than £20m. Why this range? For a start, there are many high quality, but usually expensive, legal and commercial advisers available from a number of sources in the UK (financial services companies, banks, consultants) for much larger businesses than this. Not surprisingly, access to this advice becomes more difficult the smaller the company.

In addition, there are many businesses in the UK that fall into this category. In 1999, 97 per cent of VAT registered businesses had sales revenues under £5m and 90 per cent had revenues of less than £1m.

Public Limited Companies (PLCs) are out of the scope of this book because very few small start-up businesses fall within this category and the complexities of public share ownership and stock market trading is worthy of much more in-depth analysis.

Most topics are covered in a practical way; with the topics being those most important for survival. I choose the word 'survival' because in the early years that is exactly how it will seem – a matter of life or death! Being a small business in today's complex trading world is at best difficult, at worst impossible! I have indicated those things that should be considered essential and have made suggestions on actions you should take if you are to give yourself the best chance of survival.

As the new entrepreneur soon realises, there are hundreds of decisions to make and guidance is needed on almost all of these. Most companies formed in the UK fail within the first 18 months, with more than 75 per cent never getting past three years of trading. A daunting thought, but one that has not led to a decline in the number of start-ups. In 1999 for example a record number of new companies were formed.

Unfortunately, there are very few golden rules. Evidence suggests that genuine success with a small company is as much to do with a strong will to survive and sheer drive and determination as with following a particular methodology or practice.

The average number of years between global recessions is reducing and the impact of each downturn increasing. Almost two decades elapsed between the first two recessions in post-1945 Britain, but only six years between the two most recent. Hence, proprietors need to take every appropriate measure to insulate themselves against such events.

As we enter the new millennium, we are seeing a resurgence of respect for the smaller business unit. The recent success of many .com companies, employing a few highly skilled and dedicated staff, has helped, but these are not the only success stories. Every day greater numbers of small companies are being bought. The most successful are now being sold for increasing sums for their entrepreneurial founders, having built a reputation and a strong track record for the development of niche products and skill-sets.

This book is based largely on my own personal experience, where I have successfully helped to shape small- and medium-sized, private- and publicly-owned businesses for more than a decade. The experiences have not all been good! Looking back, it is clear I made many basic mistakes, often through ignorance of the situation. Almost everyone makes the same mistakes –

and so why not describe some of the more obvious ones so that we can improve the lot of Great Britain PLC, where entrepreneurial culture is at long last alive and kicking?

Where appropriate, I have referenced national statistics, legal details and business theory. However, I have tried to lay out the issues, the pitfalls, the ups and the downs as I see them in a straightforward and frank manner in order that little is left to chance.

The main reason for writing this book is to provide really practical advice to the small business community and, wherever possible, keep away from theoretical analysis. Daily business life is not about theory. It concerns managing the forthcoming crisis that is about to befall you if you do not take action today while keeping a positive persona during preparations for the next customer presentation!

You need a very wide range of skills to be successful and you must be determined to reach the targets you set yourself. The business world we face today has never been more complex; only the fittest survive. While we all need an element of good fortune along the way, I am confident that you can greatly improve your chances of achieving the aims you set out with if you remember the four Cs:

- *Clarity*: develop your personality so that it is strong enough to overcome the down times, remains clearly focused on the business targets and is not too easily swayed by the comments of others
- *Communication*: learn how to communicate with people at any level in a clear and concise way (both orally and in writing). By this I mean interaction with people from any class, race, age group, sex or business position
- *Clear thinking*: have the necessary drive and determination to keep finding new and innovative ways to solve difficult problems and to think rationally, however emotionally charged situations become

- *Commitment*: feel the underlying desire to keep on going, however tough the going gets.

These attributes are not enough on their own but, when harnessed with some of the hints given in this book, it is my belief that you will greatly improve your chances of securing your aims.

I trust you find the text useful in building and even selling your business in the future. I would welcome your comments. Please forward these by e-mail to:
BOOKREPLY@AOL.COM.

2 Start with the end in mind

When deciding to start your own business, two of the most important decisions to make are:

- why this particular venture over another; and
- what are my short-, medium- and long-term objectives?

Getting answers to these questions will help you decide not just what business you want to be in now but also how you plan to make an exit route in the future; either when you sell the business to make a financial gain or pass it on to your children or dependants.

Why do people start their own business?

Let us start with the reasons why people choose to start their own business. There are many hundreds of these, but we can group them together under four main headings, taking account of the usual age of the owner:

- *Desire*: you may have held a quiet determination to start a company in a particular field, and circumstances have dictated that now is the right time (usually aged 18+)
- *Irritation*: if you have worked for more than enough bosses and found that you simply cannot perform under them you might decide it would be better to work for yourself (usually aged 25+)
- *Redundancy*: if alternative employment cannot be found elsewhere then you might consider starting your own company to provide an income flow (usually aged 35+)
- *Retirement*: if you have retired from a lifelong career you

might consider starting your own company to keep the mind and body active (usually aged 45 +).

At the founding of the company (and there are more than 1.6m businesses in the UK), the owners start off with a clear vision. They usually feel apprehensive, especially if this is their first attempt, but almost all new proprietors feel bullish about their new venture and cannot wait to get underway.

However, say six months later, ask them again why they started the company and what their medium- and long-term objectives are. Almost certainly, these will have been forgotten! The daily pressures of the business, the long hours, issues with suppliers, customer queries, the filling-in of value added tax (VAT) returns and the like all take their toll on the owners and their staff.

So when you start your business, make sure you clearly identify a number of short-, medium- and long-term objectives for you, your staff and the company. Make the targets difficult, but realistic, to achieve. Be sure to have plenty of them – at least ten short-, ten medium- and five long-term goals – including your personal endgame target (see Figure 1).

Two useful quick definitions are:

- *Tactical*: short-term actions or decisions (say immediate to less than six months) aimed at solving just the problem(s) in hand.
- *Strategic*: longer-term actions or decisions (usually looking at least three years ahead) aimed at creating the environment for future change.

Double creation

In his book *The Seven Habits of Highly Effective People*, Stephen Covey suggests that all things are created twice. There is a mental or first creation, and a physical or second creation to all things.

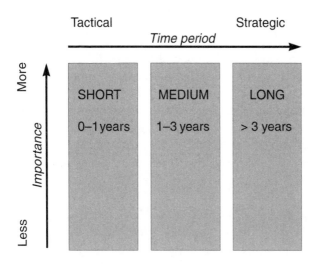

Figure 1 Define the short-, medium- and long-term business objections

He describes the building of a house from scratch where the designer has the mental creation and prepares blueprints. Following this is the creation phase or the building of the home. Building a business is exactly like this. You need to visualise exactly what you want to build, plan it and then physically create it.

Taking this further, the management and leadership of the business represent two creations. The leadership comes first. It is concerned with the high-level and overall direction of the company and needs to be clearly articulated. Management comes second. It is a bottom-line focus defining how best certain things can be accomplished.

You will need to lead your company by ensuring that all management and staff understand the vision and objectives for the business. The management process is how you will actually *get* there.

In summary – 'Management is doing things right, Leadership is doing the right things'.

Visionary companies

An extensive study by James Collins and Jerry Porras in their book *Built to Last* investigated a large number of major corporations that had been trading for more than 50 years and might be considered *visionary*. The authors wanted to find out what made these companies really successful.

They concluded that some of the most successful or *visionary* companies which have traded for more than 50 years exhibit a wide range of common traits. In particular such companies:

- *Set Big, Hairy Audacious Goals (BHAGs)*: in other words, they are not afraid to set targets which seem from the outset to be almost impossible to achieve. You must do the same. Consider it part of your role in leading the business to set one or two BHAGs for the company to chase. Ensure they are fully understood and can be measured and monitored. Include some milestones for people to celebrate reaching along the way
- *Consider 'good enough' never is*: only the best will do; accepting that something is *good enough* always results in lower standards of achievement and ultimately in a business which underperforms. In smaller companies, a *good enough* attitude will lead to missed opportunities, lost business and a culture which accepts second best
- *Preserve the core; stimulate progress*: allocating enough of your staff's precious time to search out new products or investigate new markets may often seem difficult. However, this is crucial. The modern business world is changing faster than ever before and while you must *preserve the core*, through investment in the present processes and systems, you must *stimulate progress* by creating the new products, services and markets for the medium-term future. Try 60–80 per cent in *preserve the core* and 40–20 per cent in *stimulate progress*

8

- *Consider more than profits*: *visionary* companies are not just out to maximise short-term profits. They realise that building a company or brand that customers will recognise for quality or service is more important than the immediate bottom-line.

A good example of the above points is the company Hewlett-Packard. They were not *formed* with the view of becoming one of the world's great manufacturing businesses. In fact, the early exploits of Bill Hewlett and Dave Packard produced less than sparkling results! John Young, Hewlett-Packard chief executive officer in 1992, stated 'our basic principles have endured intact since our founders conceived them. We distinguish between core values and practices; the core values don't change but the practices might. We've also remained clear that profit – as important as it is – is not why the Hewlett-Packard Company exists; it exists for more fundamental reasons' (*Built to Last*, James Collins & Jerry Porras).

What goals should I set?

These will vary depending on the type of company you are running but there should be categories of short-, medium- and long-term along with a statement of the core values you will uphold. All of your goals should pass the PASS test, namely:

- Produce a measurable result – you cannot manage something that cannot be measured
- Achievable, but with some degree of effort – only activities with some difficulty are worth achieving. However, make sure the objectives are realistic
- Simple to understand – everyone associated with the organisation, including shareholders, should be clear about the objectives

- Specific to the business you run and relevant in terms of timeframe.

Examples of each type of goal and a statement of core values might include:

- *Short*: the taking of an order for £1,000 or more within the first four weeks of trading; passing the £100,000 turnover mark within the first four months of the year
- *Medium*: securing the fiftieth new customer; having sufficient reserves to pay the first shareholders' dividend
- *Long*: securing a paper valuation (endgame) for the business of more than £0.5m; having enough business to consider employing a general manager
- *Core values*: to provide the best customer service at competitive rates (which may not always be the cheapest) using the latest technology available; always to give customers the benefit of the doubt and do what is necessary to ensure they remain loyal; to invest sufficient resources to stay abreast of new product developments; to provide management and staff with a secure working environment that breeds a culture of cooperation and sharing for the common good of the business.

The Foundation Circle

The Foundation Circle represents the structural relationship between your aims and objectives and the daily running of the business. It has three layers and can be represented as shown in Figure 2.

The *Goals and Objectives* shown in Figure 2 are the medium- and long-term aims referred to above. To achieve your *goals* successfully, you must build a suitable *Organisation Structure*. Hence if the development of a national sales force with a

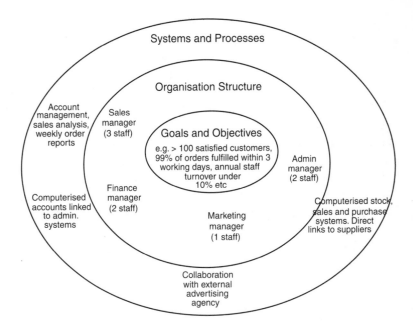

Figure 2 The Foundation Circle

strong regional presence is part of the long-term plan, you must build an appropriate company structure to support its delivery properly. Finally, well defined *Systems and Processes* must underpin everything. The systems may be manual or automated/computerised; in either case they will need to be well thought through and devised totally to support the *Organisation Structure* and the *Goals and Objectives.*

There is a natural link from the inner to the outer segments of the Foundation Circle. It is best to start with the definition of the *Goals and Objectives.* Once these are well defined and understood, move on to the *Organisation Structure* which will be required (in-house versus third-party and internal functions etc.) and finally consider the all embracing *Systems and Processes.*

11

For example, if you intend selling books or CDs over the Internet, the type of *Organisation Structure* will be totally different to that of a high-street retailer. It is likely that you will place great emphasis on the marketing of your company's image, particularly with Internet users, and on the up-time of the computer systems. Close collaboration with a number of key third-party companies, such as a logistics provider, will be essential. This implies a very different structure to the 'do everything in-house' approach of most traditional stores.

In their book *Exploring Corporate Strategy*, Gerry Johnson and Kevan Scholes pose the deceptively simple question, 'What business are we in?' They define the boundaries that managers give to their organisation in terms of geography, product or service or the way business is conducted. Setting these guides is essential as it indicates the nature of the organisation to all management and staff.

Growth of companies

There is a standard growth curve for all companies which highlights that there are periods of varying growth; starting with the initial spurt when the company is first formed, through continued expansion as it becomes more stable, to a plateau when it may even go into decline (see Figure 3).

The length of each period may vary. In practice, it may be difficult to know where your business is on the growth curve, especially once you have been trading more than a few years. However, being aware of the curve should help you accept that the issues associated with growth are quite normal and are being experienced by all other businesses.

Depending upon the commercial sector you trade in, there will be a severe period of initial volatility that could last as long as three years. Throughout this period, high rates of change will impact on everything and everyone associated with the organisation. You will be tempted to make changes to your original plans. You may even consider re-evaluating the overall direction of the company.

Unless it is a matter of survival, do *not* amend your original plans. These pressures are quite normal. The issues may not be only of a financial nature. They might also be operational. Your new company will have no established daily procedures of the type that a more mature business might have and therefore you will need to devise them, ensure they are clearly understood by all staff, and monitored.

In summary, following an initial flurry of activity during, say, the first six to nine months, your company should settle down before more rapid changes become noticeable from around 18 months onwards. During both phases, pressures will be at their peak. You will need to keep focused on the reasons why you started the business in the first place.

I will mention the growth curve later but, for now, you should note the curve indicates that the rate of change in most companies increases in intensity as the business grows. During the initial months, rapid rates of change will put severe pressure on the owners. Although the second period of growth

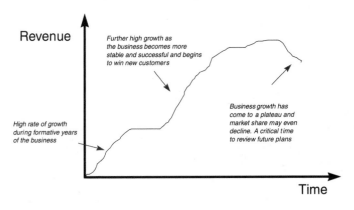

Figure 3 Business growth curve

13

may be more intense, it is likely that you and your staff will be able to contend with difficulties better the second time around. Why?

Over time, the owners and staff of small companies have to become more adaptable to change and better able to cope with the pressures of the business. This happens almost automatically and is partly to do with experience. It is also because the internal and external procedures for managing day-to-day activities become more well defined and understood as the business matures.

The endgame

Now to the endgame and the way in which you will exit from the business. At first you might ask, 'Why on earth do I need to consider how I will leave the company I have helped to form and in which I am happy?' Good question. The reason is that the timing, the dependencies and the route of your exit often determine the manner in which you run the business.

On the surface, it may appear that an exit plan is the thing furthest from the minds of the new owners. However, the plan gives direction and purpose to what may otherwise become a company that just provides the basic level of funds to meet the family's requirements and no more. All companies need to consider the major uncertainties of the future, such as if the owner cannot work or if third-party events threaten the business.

Writing an initial business plan (see chapter 4) is an essential step to defining the endgame. The plan will focus your mind on: setting the short-, medium- and long-term goals for the company; determining the supporting organisational structure; and creating the systems and processes that will be employed.

It will also force you to consider other important factors which are considered in more detail in later chapters, such as:

- how you intend winning and retaining customers
- what costs of sale you will consider acceptable
- who the target customers will be and how you will reach them
- who will be your suppliers and on what terms
- how the business will be financed
- what the ultimate exit plan will be.

There are four distinct types of endgame business, as follows:

- a family business to pass on to dependants
- an income-generating business
- a nest-egg business (up to ten years)
- a fast-growth business (less than five years).

These are now discussed in turn.

A family business to pass onto dependants

The traditional type of company, started with a view to creating wealth for future generations of the family, has its own style of endgame. This type of business will generally exhibit a smooth growth curve. The aim of most (although it has to be said not all) family business owners is not to go flat out for growth but rather to tread a more manageable and steady path, putting the right building blocks in place.

As far as the endgame is concerned, the owners should plan to cease full-time involvement with the company once it has reached a suitable size and stability and, most important, once an heir has been identified. They should plan the number of years they want (or expect) to run the business for, based on their current age and expected retirement date. By doing this, they set expectations in their own minds (and those of their financiers) for the shape of the growth curve and their likely exit date.

15

All will be fine unless they cannot find an obvious successor from the immediate family (and/or there are no willing volunteers.) If that happens, the family business owners may well find themselves needing to follow one of the other exit plans outlined below.

Family business: example

Mr and Mrs Jones decided to open a new retail store selling low-cost jewellery. They are in their late thirties and have two young children. Mr Jones is to give up his job working for a major high-street jewellery store to start the company. They will invest £30,000 of their own money and will borrow £200,000 from a bank to buy stock, pay for premises, etc.

It is the intention of the Joneses to build the company slowly. During the early years Mrs Jones will help with the bookkeeping and will work in the shop when convenient. Their plan is to retire within 20 years at which time the business will either pass on to one of their offspring, another member of the family or a third-party buyer. In each situation, Mr and Mrs Jones (and their financiers) know from the outset their plan of exit. They can determine the value they want for the business when they sell and hence determine the right growth pattern.

An income-generating business

As the name suggests, an income-generating business provides the security of regular income for the owner.

It is possible that the owner may have worked for many years in a particular field and has grown tired of working for someone else. He or she has therefore decided to go it alone. It might be that the new proprietor feels that working for others no longer gives the security they need and has decided they must be in control of their own destiny. They might, as is becoming true in an alarming number of cases, see it as the only way to guarantee work.

Income-generating business: example

Mr Brown is in his early forties and decides to start his own plumbing and heating business. This is a trade he knows well. By taking a step out on his own, Mr Brown hopes to overcome some of the financial difficulties he has faced in recent years to provide a more regular income for his family.

Mr Brown wants to retire at 60. In the period between now and then, he plans to build his business. Initially it will be just himself and a young trainee, but he would like to expand so that he has five full-time employees. These will be of different ages and experience, allowing him to keep his costs under control as he takes on more work. He is confident that with five staff he will be able to continue close supervision of the work done, but also be able to leave the business to take holidays and spend more time with his family.

On retirement, Mr Brown would like to sell his regular business contracts to another local firm, while keeping a small involvement, possibly as a consultant. If successful, Mr Brown will not only have received his regular income from the business but also a small nest-egg for his retirement.

A nest-egg business (up to ten years)

The ten-year nest-egg company is for the purposes of generating a lump sum value for retirement. It is usually started, therefore, by someone over 40 who has had experience in one or more fields of commerce.

To sell to a willing suitor within the time period, the ten-year nest-egg business must grow quickly and effectively. Over the ten years, the owners will need to establish the company, overcome one or more cyclical difficulties that hit every business (and the economy as a whole), and build a track record with which to value the company.

Nest-egg business: example

Mr Rogers is aged 45 and wants to start a new computer software company providing systems for the banking community. He would like the business to provide him with a lump sum of £500,000 after he sells it in ten years (under present taxation regulations this will be tax free as, at the time of the sale, he will be over 50 and will be retiring).

These points immediately determine the business growth curve that Mr Rogers must follow. They also determine which are the most important factors he must consider to be sure of achieving his objectives taking account of the uncertainties that will hit any company over a ten-year period – including the possibility of recession.

Given the current and expected future market trends, the prices being paid and the calculations used to value computer software businesses, it is possible for Mr Rogers to see what he must achieve to generate the business worth he requires.

The owners starting a ten-year nest-egg company do so knowing that they will exit from the company within this period and so they take all decisions in this light. They avoid leases, mortgages and other long-term commitments of more than ten years if at all possible.

There is a need for the company to grow at a fairly rapid but well-structured pace, so that there is sufficient history of trading to generate the owners a business value equal to the lump sum they require at retirement.

It is worth noting that there are special rules in the UK governing the taxation of capital gains generated by owners of businesses aged over 50 for retirement purposes. There are also new provisions (post Oct. 1999) where previous owners retain shares in the acquiring company for a period of four years or more. You should seek guidance from your accountant or financial adviser as the latest provisions, expected to change in the near future, are presently under review.

A fast-growth business (less than five years)

Last but not least, the five-year fast-growth business is similar in some respects to the ten-year nest-egg, except that there is a much shorter time period and the owners are unlikely to retire at the end.

The purpose in creating a business of this type is to take advantage of a particular niche market in which there has been, or is expected to be, a high rate of growth. In recent years, such sectors have included computer software and services, Internet-related services, call-centre management, biotechnology and hi-tech component distribution.

In this scenario, it is highly likely that external funding will be necessary to cover the business costs that will apply during the first few years of trading. At this time, cash flow is at a premium. The company may not generate any profits until its third year of

19

trading (sometimes later than this) and hence facilities will need to be in place to meet the expenses in the interim period.

Fast-growth business: example

Ms Evans has prepared a business plan to start a new Internet software company providing systems to the insurance community. She wants to build the company by attracting three or four large clients so that when she is ready to sell the business privately in five years' time, it will be able to net her around £350,000 (after taking account of the venture capital investment – the money invested into the business by a third party at the outset).

As with Mr Rogers in the ten-year nest-egg example above, the exit route she wants immediately determines the shape of the growth curve for Ms Evans to follow. However, unlike the other exit routes, with just a five-year period under consideration, she is much more likely to be able to predict the uncertainties that may hit the company.

The key to success of a fast-growth company is a clear statement of the business objectives ('the business plan') in order that progress can be carefully monitored throughout the five-year period. Fast growth companies are notoriously difficult to manage as they experience high rates of change coupled with developing internal procedures and a continually expanding workforce.

Often, with this type of business, the identity of a potential buyer is known from the outset. Assuming the owners keep to their business plan, the value of the company will be such that the various parties concerned – financiers and shareholders – will generate sufficient returns to make this high risk investment worthwhile.

In the examples above, we have considered the endgame. You must start your new company with the end clearly in mind because without knowing where you are heading is like driving a car without a purpose. The exit route is a key determinant in how you run and manage the business. It dictates the rate of growth required, how large you need to make the business and the ultimate value of the company necessary to meet your objectives.

Now let us go back to basics and define what exactly constitutes a company and what the responsibilities are of the owners, managers and directors.

Start with the end in mind checklist

1 Why am I starting this particular business and not one in another field?
2 What is my key driver (desire, irritation, redundancy, retirement)?
3 What are my short-, medium- and long-term goals for the business?
4 Have I got enough short-(ten), medium-(ten) and long-term (five) goals?
5 Do they pass the PASS test: Produce a measurable result, Achievable with some effort, Simple to understand, Specific to the business.
6 Ensure that the core objectives and values of the company are set as a yardstick for future decision-making.
7 The Foundation Circle shows the relationship between your goals, the organisational structure of the company and the underlying systems and processes which support daily activity.
8 Do not amend your original plans unless it is a matter of survival.
9 Remember, the growth curve affects small and large companies alike.
10 Strive to put internal procedures in place as soon as possible.
11 Consider what the endgame is. A family, an income-generating, a ten-year nest-egg or a five-year fast growth business?

3 What constitutes a company?

There are many different types of company. However, for the purposes of this book, these are divided into three distinct categories:

- Sole trader
- Partnership
- Private Limited Company (Ltd).

Sole trader

The sole trader, as the name suggests, is a company run by one person – the owner. The major advantage of setting up a sole trader business is that it is very easy and inexpensive to do so, and you can be up and running almost immediately. The main requirements are that you trade using separate bank accounts for your personal and business transactions and that ideally you employ an accountant or bookkeeper to prepare your financial reports.

On the downside though, there are many disadvantages. These include:

- the company growth curve is limited by the number of hours you can work
- your personal assets are at risk
- if you do not work (due to illness or holiday), you do not receive any income
- you cannot easily expand the business, as while you are working you cannot be selling and marketing
- you have no one to share your problems or successes with and it can be a lonely existence.

Given the more highly regulated business world in which we trade today, the number of sole trader businesses has declined as a percentage of all companies during the past decade. This trend is likely to continue. Also, the introduction of a number of recent UK fiscal changes (such as the IR35 legislation announced in 1999 which was aimed at reducing potential national insurance avoidance by professional services companies) and the increased requirements for government reporting has reduced the financial benefits of acting as a sole trader.

If we 'start with the end in mind', the sole trader company does little to achieve the objectives that a person may have in the long-term. As a short-term or interim step towards a larger business it is fine. However, to progress beyond the 'window cleaner' syndrome, where earning money depends on cleaning more windows, a different approach is more appropriate.

Partnerships

A partnership is a company formed by two or more people. It is almost always a non-limited trading entity and therefore the liability of the owners (or partners) is unlimited. The legislation on partnerships dates back to 1890 and there are no formal requirements for creating such a relationship.

Like the sole trader company, a partnership has the advantage of being extremely easy to set up. However, consider the following important issues before entering into such an arrangement. First, do you know your partners? Well, presumably yes, otherwise you would not be entering into such an arrangement! But how well?

- Are they financially secure?
- Do they have a stable home life (this might affect their ability to work in the future)?

24

- Do they have any skeletons from the past relevant to this venture?
- Do they have any other business interests?
- Do you hold the same views on how the business should be traded and grown?
- What are their long-term goals for the business (income generating, nest-egg or fast growth)?

When you enter into a partnership, you are agreeing personally to fund the business in the event of financial difficulty. If you intend using banks or other financial institutions to support you, they will almost certainly demand a 'joint and several guarantee' – which means that, should they need to call in a loan or overdraft, they can come to any one or more of the partners for the whole amount, not just that partner's share.

Almost everybody starts a new company with a spirit of optimism. It is a new adventure and you want to show that you have the will to succeed and make it big where others have failed. In the case of a partnership, you would do well to learn from the experts.

The 'Big 5' audit firms – Arthur Andersen, Deloitte Touche, KPMG, PriceWaterhouseCoopers and Ernst & Young – all trade as partnerships. They have extremely detailed codes of conduct for their partners and staff that determine the way in which they conduct business.

Only partners can make statements or sign documents that might expose the company to financial difficulties or litigation, and their code of practice describes in immense detail how the business is run in order that potential disputes or uncertainties can be avoided.

While you may not go to the lengths that these firms do, as they trade with large and complex multinationals, a generally agreed set of principles between the partners covering some of the areas listed below is absolutely essential as a means of avoiding difficulties in the future.

A partnership code of practice should cover:

- the policies for remuneration and profit share
- roles and responsibilities of partners and managers
- which partner will be responsible for each area of the business
- employment terms and conditions
- the employment and dismissal of staff and partners
- the feel of the business – i.e. very formal or informal in terms of attire, business practice, etc. and the general way in which matters are handled
- company goals and objectives/the core values for the business
- the business plan and growth curve for the firm and whether it will be traded as income generating, nest-egg or fast growth
- sales and marketing plans
- commercial trading terms
- how changes to the constitution or code of practice are managed
- the financing of the business including risk and reward.

As you can see, it does not take long before a wide range of subjects, from how the partnership is formed to how it will trade and how it might be dissolved, are covered by the code of practice. It would be worth drafting a copy between yourselves and then having a legal representative make some comments.

From the outset you can quickly and easily resolve many potential issues (before they become major difficulties) for the sake of a few thousand pounds in legal fees. The golden rule is to consider every type of difficult 'what if' scenario. However negative this might seem, putting in place the correct legal framework today to cover the problems you might have tomorrow is much safer and cheaper in the long term.

Partnership business: example

Three partners, supplying local companies with computer-based terminals, had no such code of practice. One of them was responsible for securing new business; the other two for installing and maintaining the systems thereafter. During the three years they had traded, the company progressed well and the partners were enjoying reasonable rewards. At the start of the fourth year, the sales partner secured a very large piece of business that she decided was too good to share. She promptly announced she was leaving and going her own way, taking her new order with her. Given the cost of fighting the wayward partner through the courts, which would have been prohibitively expensive without any written agreement to base it on, the other two partners decided to simply carry on and find another more suitable partner to support the business. This time, they drew up a code of practice from the start.

In all cases, there will be a fine balance between the interests of the individual and those of the business. Figure 1 indicates that as the boundaries between personal and partnership issues grow closer, so the tendency for resistance or conflict grows; rather like the physics principle that like forces repel.

Private Limited Company

The limited company is the most common of all business types and, in 1999, more than 1.5m companies were active in the UK. Companies House registers every company, usually via agents or accountants. You simply select a 'shell' company with which to start trading. Most of these have very strange names but, for a small registration fee, you can rename them as something more relevant to your own business and, as long

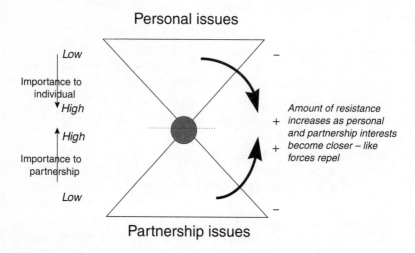

Figure 1 Balancing personal and partnership issues

as no one else has chosen that name, you can be up and running within a week or so.

When a limited company is formed, you must produce a number of essential pieces of documentation and follow certain procedures.

- Every company must have at least one director and one company secretary. These must be different people as the courts view one-person management unfavourably.
- Every company must have a Memorandum of Association (MoA) and Articles of Association (AoA). The MoA outlines a company's constitution and denotes the scope of a company's powers. It defines how you will do business with the outside world. The AoA relate to the internal regulations for the management of the business and cover some of the issues described above for a code of practice in partnerships. They detail the rights of the directors and

shareholders and set out the way in which the company must conduct its affairs.

- Every company must have an initial share capital. Most are formed with £100, although the legal minimum is actually £1. The larger the share capital of the company, the more scope there is for the issuing of shares and the better the company will be viewed by financial institutions.

- Private limited companies have two distinct interest groups: shareholders and directors. In a very small company, these parties are often one and the same. However, they need not be. Shareholders put up the initial capital to form the company and it is to them that the directors will go should additional funds be required to support the business. The shareholders appoint the directors to run the company on their behalf. Directors must know and understand the powers contained within the AoA. Their first task after being appointed should be to study these in order that they might determine how they will interact with the other directors of the company and the shareholders.

- Financial returns, at the very least showing details of the profit and loss statement and company balance sheet, must sent to Companies House each year. Anyone can view these for a small fee.

- Every year the company must hold a general or shareholders' meeting. There should be less than 15 months between meetings. If you fail to hold such a meeting, all of the directors can be liable for a fine. However, especially where the shareholders and directors are one and the same, you can dispense with the need to hold an annual general meeting by passing an 'elective resolution' for the year in question.

The private limited company represents an ideal vehicle for most smaller businesses. Recent government legislation has made it easier for small companies to file documents at Companies House and has reduced the amount of detail required. However, unlike a partnership that can keep its affairs completely private, a limited company has to make public its financial position every year.

Distinguishing factors

By way of trying to encapsulate many of the points described above, Table 1 indicates some of the important distinguishing factors between sole traders, partnerships and limited companies.

Table 1 Distinguishing factors

Distinguishing feature	Sole Trader	Partnership	Limited Company
Limited liability	No	No	Yes[1]
Separate legal entity[2]	No	No	Yes
Separation of management/ownership[3]	No	No	Yes/No
Security of financial data[4]	Yes	Yes	No

Notes
1 Limited to the assets of the company – i.e. the maximum amount (except in cases of fraud) an owner can lose is the capital of the business.
2 Whether or not the company can enter into legal activity against a third party on its own.
3 In a limited company, the directors and shareholders need not be the same.
4 Limited companies must prepare and file annual trading statements and returns with Companies House every year.

Which type of company should I choose?

A lot depends upon the commercial sector in which you will trade. The sole trader has traditionally been the domain of traders but, as stated earlier, once your company gets to a certain size where there is too much work for one person, this is probably not the best route.

The partnership suits professional firms, such as lawyers, accountants and consultants, because it is often necessary to keep details about the affairs of the company, the fees paid to its partners and its client information, out of the public domain. As there is no need to lodge the annual returns at Companies House, this protects partnerships. Just about everyone else uses a limited company.

What constitutes a company? checklist

1 Choose between one of the three types of business: sole trader, partnership or limited company. In almost all cases it will be the latter.
2 Make sure you clearly define the terms on which you will conduct business – with shareholders, customers and staff.
3 Thoroughly investigate the affairs of any potential business partner – do not just assume everything told to you is correct or true!
4 Use a lawyer to draw up any contractual documents, such as standard terms and conditions of trading or a partnership code of practice.
5 If you start a limited company, read the MoA and AoA and make sure they concur with how you see trading will take place. MoA refers to how you will do business with the outside world and AoA are for internal regulation.

4 Financing the business

Whatever type of company you decide to form, the business financing is one of the most important factors in determining whether or not you will achieve your objectives. Unfortunately, experience indicates that many businesses commence with far too little finance secured. This forces the owners to make difficult decisions regarding the future of the business, often at the most inappropriate time.

The purpose of this chapter is to outline some of the steps you can take to minimise your exposure to financial insecurity and some of the controls you can put in place to stay in touch with the development of the business; from the perspective of profit, cash flow and capital expenditure analysis.

This may sound rather technical and complex but do not be put off as the procedures noted should, within a short period of time, become second nature to you. They are essential if you are to expand the company in the future. Remember, investing in controls and practices today will reap benefits many times over tomorrow.

Have enough finance for at least Year 1

The best advice that can be given to every small company director/partner is to have enough finance available so that, should there be no income during the first year of trading, the company will survive. This may seem to be overkill but think about the alternatives.

You have invested sufficient cash into the company so that it can run for the first three months. After six weeks of trading you are struggling to secure enough regular sales income to cover your costs. What do you do? Well presumably, try to cut costs in order that you can extend your company's life. In reality, this is the opposite of what you need to do when trying to get the business off the ground!

During the first year or so, you will have a lot of unusual, unexpected and unplanned expenditure. Figure 1 depicts the likely position in Year 1 with costs being much higher than income. With the best planning in the world, there are always unforeseen or hidden expenses and it always takes a lot longer than you expect to close new sales. Waste-paper bins are full of sales forecasts predicting year-end sales results three times the level they will reach in reality!

Therefore, get the largest buffer from the outset. A cover of one year is ideal because it gives you the time you will need to overcome those inevitable difficulties and delays that are part of everyday *new business* life. Hopefully, it should mean you can avoid making drastic cutbacks or changes to your plans.

Ask for more finance when you do not need it

You have invested some of your own money and got the business started. When should you begin asking for further lines of credit?

Figure 1   Likely position in Year 1

Answer – when you are least in need of them! Why? Because if the company is buoyant, and your forecasts show that you are trading either on or above the budgets set, banks and other financial institutions will have no hesitation in meeting your requests, often on very favourable terms.

Under these conditions, you are in a position where you can take your time and play one lender or investor off against the other. You have the time to consider different types of credit line – overdrafts, bank loans, factoring, venture capital etc. and these can be negotiated to suit your needs.

You can put the facilities in place and only call on them when needed. This might not be for six months or a year hence; but you look all the more professional because you are planning ahead of time.

Take the counter position, where you only attempt to get funds when you need them. Now you are under time pressures, the figures do not look so healthy and you must fight to get terms and conditions that seem even half reasonable to you. The likelihood is that, if you can get credit at all, it will be on much less favourable terms and with conditions that might penalise either you or the business in the future.

So in all cases, ask for the lines of credit when trade is good, not bad! You do not have to draw them down at that point, but this ensures that you have put in place sufficient funds secure in the knowledge that you have something to fall back on in the event of difficulties.

But where should you get finance for the business from? Once you have exhausted your own financial reserves, there are generally two options open to you. The first is either a loan or an overdraft from the bank; the second is to give up part of the shares in the business in return for investment. In some circumstances, you may need a combination of the two.

Bank finance

The modern banking community is vastly different to that which operated up to the late 1980s when the small business trader was often seen as an irritation and horror stories filled pages of the daily newspapers. The adage then was: 'beware the banker that lends you an umbrella when the sun is shining but takes it away when it rains'. Today you are likely to find specialist advisers; these staff are trained in issues facing small and medium sized companies and should be sympathetic to your needs.

The initial meeting to discuss your financing will be very important, with both sides looking to make a strong impression. Personal chemistry is often as important as a good business case. It will be essential that each party has a clear understanding of the other's business issues and appreciates the potential risks to either side.

For your part, you should expect the bank to demonstrate their understanding of, and enthusiasm for, your business before deciding whether to look elsewhere. This will be a key factor in your determining whether to give them your custom. Assuming you have done your homework and have prepared a suitable business plan (see below), it should be possible to negotiate favourable terms for the financing.

Generally, although a bank is looking for a satisfactory return, its primary concern is likely to be the security of the funds it is advancing. Hence, you will need to prepare a report which will allow them to assess the likely risks. Banks tend not to like unwelcome surprises! Hence, allowing them to analyse all of the risks associated with the support of your company is a better way to create a lasting relationship than not highlighting certain issues.

The business plan will provide you with a chance to demonstrate your ability accurately to articulate the goals and focus of the company and produce well crafted management reports and forecasts. The bank's primary focus is likely to be on earnings, cash flow and how much capital is required. But, at the very least, the business plan should include the following information:

- Executive summary
- Introduction to the company
- Products, services and competition
- Markets and marketing
- Management and personnel
- Risk factors and rewards
- Financial information (including income and expenditure and cash flow forecasts for the next three years and current invested capital – see Equity finance below).

The terms and conditions for either a bank loan or overdraft facility will depend largely upon your ability to persuade and the strength of the business plan. However, other factors, such as the strength of the management team and the stability of earnings, are also likely to play a major part in the bank's viewpoint, as these will directly influence the risk.

As for how much you might be able to borrow, the lender will want to be satisfied that there is enough asset cover for the amount being lent. This might mean your shareholders and you providing security, but the bank will want to be sure that the chances of calling this in are low.

A measure used widely by banks is interest cover. As a rule of thumb, most would like to see, in the first year of trading, their interest charges covered more than twice by the operating profits. They will also expect to see a cash flow forecast which will not overburden or constrain the company.

Equity finance

As the name suggests, equity finance involves finding someone prepared to take shares in your company in return for an investment.

There are many different types of equity financiers, ranging from wealthy individuals looking to make their funds work harder, to business angels specialising in investments in high-growth entrepreneurs, to venture capitalists looking for larger opportunities (usually more than £500,000).

There are varying stages of equity finance. The first investment phase is known as 'seed capital'. This is the funding required to get the business off the ground and is usually covered by the shareholders in the business. In unusual circumstances, where the initial investment required to start the company is very high, outside seed capital might be forthcoming – but it is very difficult to raise.

The second and subsequent rounds of finance are similar to the first phase. Wealthy individuals, business angels and venture capitalists have a desire to exchange their cash for your shares and, by this stage, they will have a track record to base their investment decision upon.

As with bank finance, the potential investors need to sell to you as much as vice versa. The most important long-term asset you hold in your company is shares – so by giving some of these up in return for cash now, you are diluting your eventual payout when the company is sold. So be careful and vigilant. The process of raising equity finance can be long and drawn out and is not for the faint-hearted!

The process of raising equity finance is like bank finance. You will need to prepare a business plan similar to the one outlined above, indicating clearly how much funding is required and over what timescale. This will require you to prepare a detailed cash flow forecast indicating how much capital is required in total and when this will need to be drawn down.

One major difference between bank and equity financing is that the latter usually wish to exit from the business within five years, sometimes as soon as three. This will have a major impact upon your business. After five years you should be

38

starting to expand quite rapidly and the one thing you will need most is access to funds.

Before actually making a decision on which equity partner to choose, it is helpful to lay out the criteria upon which the judgement will be based. Use the checklist below during your meetings with different potential partners and develop the questions around these various topics:

- *Financial objectives*: what do they want from the transaction? When do they want to exit from your company?
- *Size of transaction*: how does the amount of money you want compare to their normal size of investment? If it is much smaller or larger than the average, you may find the potential partner unable to give this their best attention.
- *Funds available*: how much in total do they have available to invest? You should know this in case you, or other companies they have investments in, need more in the future.
- *Type of deal*: is the money being invested to be exchanged fully for shares or partly in shares and partly as a loan – *mixed debt and equity* financing?
- *Sector experience*: how much do they know about the market in which you trade? If there are some special issues facing you then they will need to be sympathetic to these.
- *Method of decision-making*: who will make the decision as to whether you can have the funds? Who else do you need to influence? You may want to press for a meeting with everyone who potentially has a hand in determining your future!
- *Post-investment relationship*: how will they manage their investment in your company once the deal is struck? Do they want to put someone on the board of directors or appoint the chairman? Under what circumstances might they be able to call in the present, or withhold further, funding?
- *Other factors*: do you trust these people? Remember, you are giving up your most valuable asset (shares) in order to

get short-term funds, and those you are dealing with must have integrity.

The best way to find a venture capitalist is by personal recommendation. It is likely that many of the businesses you deal with, or colleagues in the local trade association, will have used equity finance at some stage. Your accountant will also have clients that could recommend either individuals or venture capital companies.

If you are not satisfied with, or are unable to make progress in this way, then try the *British Venture Capital Association* (BVCA) *Directory of Members*. This gives a brief profile of each firm and the key things they are looking for. For much smaller transactions, the BVCA also publishes the *Directory of Business Angels*. This is for transactions requiring less than £500,000.

Once you have found a potential equity partner, try to get the first appointment at your own premises. This will help to give you more confidence. However, most venture capital companies will resist this as their time is limited.

Plan no longer than an hour for the first meeting. Expect to present a brief summary of the company, your goals and objectives for the next three years, the most important traits of the market in which you trade and some information about the products and services you supply. If possible, take along two or three of your most senior staff.

Most important of all, keep the presentation brief and to the point. You will be grilled on the financial aspects of your plans, so rehearse with your colleagues the type of difficult questions that might be asked, and ensure you have some good responses prepared.

Write a budget and stick to it

When running a small company, it is very easy to omit one essential piece of business practice; using proper budgetary controls. Why? Because most small companies prefer chasing after every piece of new business they encounter and see the writing of a budget (at the start of the year) and a forecast (each month as the year progresses) as of no real benefit to them.

Most owners argue they know the income and expenditure levels. Why bother to write them down as that is what the company accountant does each month when she or he prepares the management accounts.

Not true! Budgets and forecasts provide you with an easy to read picture of the business you have secured to date and that which you expect to achieve in the rest of the present financial year. On the positive front, you do not need to possess any specialist accounting knowledge to read or understand a budget or forecast. You do not need to appreciate the difference between accruals, prepayments and/or the provisions for depreciation!

What you see in a budget or forecast is financial information in its raw form and, if you prepare your computer-based models correctly, you can make changes to the projections, allowing you to perform 'what-if' analyses.

Without an original budget, and the subsequently revised monthly forecasts, your business is like a ship without a compass or a car without a journey planner. You are sailing aimlessly. You know little of the detail of where you are going to or where you came from – even if you do have an overall idea of the target location.

The budgetary process

Regiment the budgetary process. Start by making a list of all of the major cost areas in which the company will make expenditure: salaries, rent, rates, travel, subsistence, expenses etc.; and then allocate the amount you expect to spend under each heading month by month for the fiscal year. Be as accurate as you can. Check the renewal dates for policies. See if there are likely to be inflationary increases and apply them.

Do the same for the income lines. Ideally you should break these down into the major activities of the company so that you can monitor how each part of the business is performing (e.g. new direct sales, new third-party or dealer sales, maintenance and support contract income).

The first time you collate the information, expect many weeks of toil! However, each time you come to revise the figures, the amount of time taken will reduce and slowly the process will become part of your monthly routine. Get some help and advice from your accountant or financial adviser and use suitable computer-based spreadsheet packages (such as Microsoft Excel or Lotus 1-2-3) to keep the figures up to date.

In large private companies and PLCs, the staff within the accounts department spend many months preparing the annual budget and then several days every month preparing revised forecasts in order that senior managers and directors know the position of the business in relation to that expected.

Types of budget and forecast

There are many types of budget and forecast. The three main types we shall consider are:

- Income and expenditure
- Cash flow
- Capital expenditure.

Of these, the most important to start with is the income and expenditure. Each month, the income and expenditure forecast becomes more accurate showing the actual sales you have secured, the costs you have incurred in previous months and a projection of those you will make in the rest of the year. The forecast also shows the predicted net profit for the present financial year.

By taking the income and expenditure forecast and then correctly phasing the timing of payments to/from suppliers/customers, you can create a cash flow forecast. It is worth noting that the income and expenditure forecast you generate each month is the platform for determining the profitability, and the potential cash exposure (via the cash flow forecast), of the company.

Completing the picture, a capital expenditure budget contains predictions for future replacement costs for capital items such as cars, computers, freezers, specialist tools etc.

So what does a spreadsheet look like and how is it best to construct it for your business? Table 1 represents a typical departmental budget forecast. Consolidation of the departmental budgets (in this case administration) produces the overall company-wide targets.

The first point to note is that this is a forecast rather than a true budget, as it highlights the current view of the business to the year-end. The values for the first three months of the year are actuals. The other nine months are either the values lifted from the original budget or the current best estimate of how the business will perform to the end of year.

The report allows you to see instantly how the administration department is performing in relation to the original budget. In particular, look at the variance column (it is often useful to indicate the percentage variance too).

The advantages of using departmental spreadsheets to analyse your business are:

- It allows you to delegate sections of the company to various managers, safe in the knowledge that they have an interest in achieving the overall targets. You are much more likely to get the full support for achieving the figures

Table 1 A typical department budget forecast

Income and Expenditure Forecast dated 1 April 2000

Printed for Administration Department

	Actual Jan	Actual Feb	Actual Mar	Forecast Apr	Forecast May	Forecast Jun	Forecast Jul	Forecast Aug to Dec	Forecast Total	Budget Total	Variances
Salaries & Wages											
- Salaries	£32,590	£29,955	£32,689	£29,555	£28,263	£29,563	£30,123	£145,774	£358,512	£360,125	£1,613
- Overtime	£1,245	£0	£0	£150	£200	£210	£0	£330	£2,135	£1,500	-£635
- NI and other taxes	£3,536	£3,130	£3,416	£3,104	£2,974	£3,111	£3,148	£15,268	£37,687	£37,790	£103
- Bonuses	£0	£0	£0	£0	£0	£1,500	£0	£1,000	£2,500	£3,000	£500
- Consultants	£0	£0	£0	£0	£0	£0	£0	£0	£0	£0	£0
- Recruitment fees	£0	£0	£0	£500	£0	£0	£500	£1,000	£2,000	£2,000	£0
- Contract & Temps	£725	£0	£0	£650	£0	£0	£650	£1,475	£3,500	£3,250	-£250
Total	£38,096	£33,085	£36,105	£33,959	£31,437	£34,384	£34,421	£164,847	£406,334	£407,665	£1,331
Other Admin Costs											
- Advertising and PR	£0	£0	£0	£675	£675	£675	£675	£3,375	£6,075	£8,100	£2,025
- Rail Fares /Car costs	£247	£297	£265	£282	£282	£282	£282	£1,410	£3,347	£3,384	£37
- Auditors	£0	£0	£0	£0	£0	£0	£0	£3,000	£3,000	£5,000	£2,000
- Entertainment	£50	£0	£65	£75	£75	£75	£75	£375	£790	£900	£110
- Postage/Stationery	£192	£186	£192	£200	£200	£200	£200	£1,000	£2,370	£2,400	£30
- Telephone/fax	£0	£0	£1,756	£750	£750	£750	£750	£3,750	£8,506	£9,000	£494
- Courier costs	£86	£25	£25	£100	£100	£100	£100	£500	£1,036	£1,200	£164
- Office equipment	£425	£425	£425	£425	£425	£425	£425	£2,125	£5,100	£5,100	£0
- S/Ware maintenance	£100	£100	£100	£100	£100	£100	£100	£500	£1,200	£1,200	£0
Total	£1,100	£1,033	£2,828	£2,607	£2,607	£2,607	£2,607	£16,035	£31,424	£36,284	£4,860
Total for Admin	£39,196	£34,118	£38,933	£36,566	£34,044	£36,991	£37,028	£180,882	£437,758	£443,949	£6,191

and the overall objectives of the department if those
managers responsible for making the targets are part of the
process of setting them
- It allows you to home in on sections of the business that
  may be under- or over-performing
- It allows you to compare the performance of different
  departments and to determine those factors that affect
  some managers more than others
- It makes the process of preparing a company-wide budget/
  target much easier
- As the year progresses, it allows you to quickly and accurately monitor whether you can afford to undertake certain
  courses of action.

By constructing the spreadsheet software package to consoli-
date all of the various departmental values, it is possible to
generate values for the company as a whole. It is usual to show
less detail in the company summary sheet than the departmental version (see Table 2).

The overall company income and expenditure forecast
shown in Table 2 indicates that company ABC is largely on
target in relation to sales but is not keeping its costs under
control.

The culprit departments for potential overspend appear to be
general overheads and research and development. Without
some changes, the forecast indicates the year-end net profit
being reduced by almost £7,000 against a budget of more than
£41,000 (i.e. a net shortfall of 17.14 per cent).

The owner can now immediately use the spreadsheet package
to undertake some fine tuning in relation to the remaining
months of the year – increasing sales and/or reducing expenditure.

Imagine your cash flow is tight. Why? It could be that sales
revenue is lower than expected, or expenditure is running
ahead and you have a stock build-up situation, or suppliers are

Table 2 Company summary sheet

Income and Expenditure Forecast dated 1 April 2000

Printed for Company ABC

	Actual Jan	Actual Feb	Actual Mar	Forecast Apr	Forecast May	Forecast Jun	Forecast Jul	Forecast Aug to Dec	Forecast Total	Budget Total	Percentage Variances
Total Sales	£69,678	£95,111	£78,956	£77,800	£80,123	£71,100	£72,100	£347,990	£892,858	£896,778	-0.44%
Cost of Sales	£3,406	£3,130	£3,416	£3,088	£2,953	£3,089	£3,148	£15,233	£37,463	£37,633	-0.45%
Expenses:											
Administration	£39,196	£34,118	£38,933	£36,566	£34,044	£36,991	£37,028	£180,882	£437,758	£443,792	-1.36%
Research & Developt	£14,400	£14,987	£12,950	£12,500	£12,500	£12,500	£12,500	£62,500	£154,837	£150,000	3.22%
Sales & Marketing	£16,245	£15,112	£14,600	£15,665	£14,960	£15,200	£15,666	£78,330	£185,778	£187,992	-1.18%
General Overheads	£4,980	£2,245	£7,866	£3,040	£3,400	£3,200	£3,020	£15,000	£42,751	£36,000	18.75%
Total	£74,821	£66,462	£74,349	£67,771	£64,904	£67,891	£68,214	£336,712	£821,124	£817,784	0.41%
Operating Income	-£8,549	£25,519	£1,191	£6,941	£12,266	£120	£738	-£3,955	£34,271	£41,361	-17.14%

pressing you for payment faster than customers are paying you. How can you tell which of these is the reason?

Your monthly accounts will provide some indications but they will not provide a complete analysis – because this is not their purpose. However, the monthly income and expenditure and cash flow forecasts, on the other hand, will provide clearer indications of where the problems lie.

Which spreadsheet do most people use?

During the last decade or so, the number of competing packages has reduced and now Microsoft Excel is the undisputed market leader.

For almost all small business users, this package should have enough facilities and features to add real value. In practice, most people use under 20 per cent of the product's capability!

The software integrates with the other Microsoft products (e.g. Word word-processing and Powerpoint presentations) as

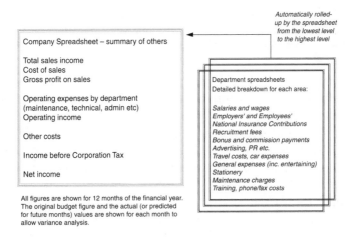

Figure 2   Overview of how a spreadsheet is constructed

part of the Office suite meaning you can produce professional-looking reports for financiers.

However, make sure you get enough training. Unless you know how to get the most out of the package, you will always be relying upon someone else to produce figures for you. In today's IT literate world, you must be able to use the tools yourself!

What's in it for me?

So what important benefits can you, as a small company owner, expect from budgeting using a computerised spreadsheet?

- *Tools to make company forecasting easier*: one advantage of using a computer-based spreadsheet for the production of income and expenditure and cash flow forecasts is that you can sit in your own office, make simple changes to the model and instantly see the results.
- *To indicate how long before you go out of business or can begin to celebrate*: the income and expenditure forecast shows whether you need to make any drastic changes to the underlying cost structure of the business in order to avoid year-end losses; and it shows you now! The corresponding cash flow forecast also indicates the likelihood of your company needing additional funds – and exactly *when* they will be needed.
- *To highlight those areas where you are spending ahead of budget*: it is good practice to check for percentage variances against the original budget. Give yourself leeway in certain months (to allow for exceptional items) but always try to keep the variances well under control in the year-end figures (no more than, say, 10 per cent against budget).
- *Better powers of delegation*: armed with departmental income and expenditure forecasts, you can give your

department heads their own models to work within. A detailed forecast means they have enough scope with which to make their own decisions while remaining bound within the overall cost constraints you have laid down in the full forecast. You can monitor progress at least on a monthly basis, being sure to ask for, and get, the reasons for exceptional items.

It is always easy to assume that the controls imposed by budgets and forecasts are unnecessary, especially when the business is small and tightly controlled. However, if introduced from an early stage, these tools can become the lifeblood of the business, enabling you to predict the highs and lows of the company more easily. They allow delegation from an early stage.

Financing the business checklist

1 Ideally, only start the business if you have enough funds to support one year of costs without income.

2 Budgets are written for the start of a new financial year. Major types are income and expenditure, cash flow and capital expenditure.

3 Forecasts (also three types) use the base budget data showing the actuals for months already traded and revised expectations to the financial year-end.

4 Write the budget and then aim to stick to it.

5 Delegate responsibility to managers and give them targets to work to by providing them with a departmental budget. Get them involved in writing the budget to get their full support for the values.

6 Computerised spreadsheets are essential as they:

- provide tools to make forecasting easier
- indicate how long before you go out of business or can begin to celebrate
- highlight those areas where you are spending ahead of budget
- provide better powers of delegation.

7 Only ask for finance when you do not need it. When the business is trading well, seek new sources of credit that can be drawn down at a future date.

8 Write a business plan to support the process of financing the business.

9 Consider debt and/or equity finance as ways of expanding the capital base of the company.

5   Cash flow is everything

In the previous chapter, we considered the financing of the business and the use of spreadsheet models to determine the present and predict the future. However, perhaps the most critical factor to note from the use of these models is the importance of timing in cash flow forecasts (as opposed to income and expenditure), and how this can virtually make or break your company.

If you get the cash flow for your business wrong, it will not only make it difficult for you to trade; it is possible that you could go out of business even though, on paper, you appear to have a successful company making profits.

How can it be possible that a company trading with profits can go under? It is all down to the timing of payments and receipts, the terms of trading (for paying suppliers and receiving cash from customers) and the dreaded sales tax in the UK and Europe, VAT. While these may sound like minor points, do not underestimate their impact.

The simplest way to highlight the size of the issue is through an example. But first some assumptions.

Cash flow model

Let us begin by assuming that you have just started a new company that is able to buy products readily and sell them to cash-paying customers both directly and through a local agent. Selling directly you make the respectable margin of 40 per cent; you give up a further 5 per cent when selling via a third party.

You need to buy stock for which you must pay cash on delivery (as you are a start-up business), with the stock being delivered a few days before it is sold. The marketing effort is also paid in advance. There is a delay between the sale of the goods and the receipt of cash from your customers of, on average, 45 days. You need to pay the three staff you employ at the end of each week. Being a careful proprietor, you set aside the National Insurance contributions on their salaries each week by transferring cash into a separate bank account.

You have estimated that you need £15,000 of financing. The figure is based on quick calculations you made using an income and expenditure spreadsheet similar to those shown in the previous chapter. Let us now have a look at the basic income and expenditure model for the start-up business (see Table 1).

The income and expenditure model shows a healthy business, almost breaking even within the first four months of

Table 1 Income and expenditure model

Income and expenditure forecast

	Month 1	Month 2	Month 3	Month 4
Income				
Sales - direct	£0	£2,250	£4,650	£6,970
Sales - third party	£0	£900	£3,100	£4,450
Total sales	£0	£3,150	£7,750	£11,420
Expenditure				
Cost of direct sales	£0	£1,350	£2,790	£4,182
Cost of third party sls	£0	£585	£2,015	£2,893
Staff (includes NI)	£4,313	£4,313	£4,313	£4,313
Marketing	£3,500	£2,500	£750	£750
Total expenditure	£7,813	£8,748	£9,868	£12,137
Net Profit	-£7,813	-£5,598	-£2,118	-£717
Cumulative Net Profit	-£7,813	-£13,410	-£7,715	-£2,835

trading and requiring around £13,500 of financial assistance. It could be safely assumed that, beyond the period in question, the general expansion of the business will see increases in both income and expenditure but that the healthy margins generated by the company will result in good ongoing profits.

But what of the cash? Does the company need any more than the £13,410? It can safely be assumed so to meet the difference in timings between sales and purchases, but how much more? Will the estimate of £15,000 be enough?

While there is no exact science, best practice suggests the cash requirement may be up to twice that indicated in the income and expenditure forecasts. You can clearly improve matters by buying on credit terms and selling for cash, but there will remain the issue of financing VAT and immovable direct costs (such as rent, rates and salaries). Your cash flow forecast may therefore look something like Table 2.

There you have it! Based on the assumptions given at the start of the chapter and after taking account of the opening £15,000 cash facility, the cash flow spreadsheet still highlights a shortfall in cash by the end of the fourth month (when the business is about to start making profits) of almost as much as was borrowed in the first place!

So in terms of financing the business, you can be making profits but go under solely because of cash flow. Most large companies have teams of staff working on improving their cash position by slowing down payments to their creditors (often to small businesses) and chasing for prompt payment of invoices. While size matters in bullying debtors to pay up (particularly the threat of withdrawing future supplies), another simple yet very effective method is to offer a small settlement discount for paying early.

This method can pay big dividends. To highlight the effectiveness, let us suppose that you agree to give buyers a 2 per cent discount in return for payment within 14 days (see Table 3). How does this alter the amount of cash required in the

Table 2 Cash flow forecast (1st version)

	Wks 1/2	Wks 3/4	Wks 5/6	Wks 7/8	Wks9/10	Wks11/12	Wks13/14	Wks15/16
Opening Cash	£15,000	£8,731	£6,575	£344	-£2,949	-£5,108	-£10,087	-£6,365
Income (inc VAT)								
VAT Reclaim							£1,810	
Sales - direct	£0	£0	£0	£0	£2,644	£0	£5,464	£0
Sales - third party	£0	£0	£0	£0	£1,058	£0	£3,643	£0
Total income	£0	£0	£0	£0	£3,701	£0	£10,916	£0
Expenditure (inc VAT)								
Cost of direct sales	£0	£0	£793	£793	£1,639	£1,639	£2,457	£2,457
Cost of third party sls	£0	£0	£344	£344	£1,184	£1,184	£1,700	£1,700
Staff (includes NI)	£2,156	£2,156	£2,156	£2,156	£2,156	£2,156	£2,156	£2,156
Marketing	£4,113	£0	£2,938	£0	£881	£0	£881	£0
Total expenditure	£6,269	£2,156	£6,231	£3,293	£5,860	£4,979	£7,194	£6,313
Closing Cash	£8,731	£6,575	£344	-£2,949	-£5,108	-£10,087	-£6,365	-£12,678
Assumed VAT rate %	17.50							

Table 3 Cash flow forecast (2nd version)

	Wks 1/2	Wks 3/4	Wks 5/6	Wks7/8	Wks9/10	Wks11/12	Wks13/14	Wks15/16
Opening Cash	£15,000	£8,731	£6,575	£344	£679	-£5,182	-£1,237	-£7,940
Income (inc VAT)								
VAT Reclaim							£491	
Sales - direct	£0	£0	£0	£2,591	£0	£5,354	£0	£8,026
Sales - third party	£0	£0	£0	£1,036	£0	£3,570	£0	£5,124
Total income	£0	£0	£0	£3,627	£0	£8,924	£491	£13,150
Expenditure (inc VAT)								
Cost of direct sales	£0	£0	£793	£793	£1,639	£1,639	£2,457	£2,457
Cost of third party sls	£0	£0	£344	£344	£1,184	£1,184	£1,700	£1,700
Staff (includes NI)	£2,156	£2,156	£2,156	£2,156	£2,156	£2,156	£2,156	£2,156
Marketing	£4,113	£0	£2,938	£0	£881	£0	£881	£0
Total expenditure	£6,269	£2,156	£6,231	£3,293	£5,860	£4,979	£7,194	£6,313
Closing Cash	£8,731	£6,575	£344	£679	-£5,182	-£1,237	-£7,940	-£1,102
Assumed VAT rate %	17.50							

example above? Do you still need an additional £12,678 overdraft facility or can you reduce this?

You now only need a £7,940 overdraft facility, and that reduces to £1,102 by the fourth month (mainly due to the cash from sales made in month four being available to the business much earlier).

But surely you are giving away profit just to finance the business? Not true! If you calculate the direct cost of twisting the arms of your customers in this way versus paying the bank or other financial institution a much higher interest charge for an overdraft/bank loan, it is no contest.

Other ways to improve cash flow

There are several other ways of improving cash flow besides offering would-be bribes to your customers through a settle-ment discount!

If we begin by looking at the cost side, you could discuss with your marketing company an element of 'at risk' money for their campaign. Let us suppose you ask for 10 per cent of your investment to be held back. Assuming the campaign is successful and delivers say, 25 per cent or even 40 per cent more than expected, you will pay a further 10 per cent to them; a 90 per cent versus 110 per cent bet. The balance of their invoice will be paid either in three months or at the end of the promotion. These simple measures combine to give you a considerable cash flow improvement.

Staff costs are more difficult. However here too, suggesting an amount of 'at risk' salary, mainly but not exclusively for your sales team, should be considered. A 20 per cent personal and a 5 per cent company bonus might provide enough incen-tive, especially if these allow you to exceed your sales revenue targets while meeting the profit forecast. They will also assist in the promotion of the entrepreneurial spirit!

It is not advisable to finance your company by assuming that pay-as-you-earn (PAYE) and National Insurance payments, which become due to the Inland Revenue each month, are additional cash flow. The same applies to VAT. Best practice is to set aside these monthly payments away from your main bank trading account in order that they can be paid promptly. Recent legislation has given powers to the tax authorities to impose punitive sanctions on late payers.

Suppliers can be surprisingly accommodating to small companies if they hold the view that they are likely to become a long-term customer. So use your powers of persuasion on them! You should not just sell to customers but to suppliers too. Without necessarily building a fantasy story, outline the potential you have to provide the supplier with a new revenue stream. As a smaller company, be bold and ask for more discount and demand longer to pay (e.g. 40 per cent on the first ten orders or £10,000 of purchases instead of the usual 20 per cent). But whatever you demand of your suppliers, be sure to keep your side of the bargain and pay on time. It will give you more scope for demanding favours in the future.

Finally, on the cost side, do not forget the costs of finding and employing new staff. It is not unusual to pay 15 to 20 per cent to recruitment agencies to locate your stars of the future. With this level of investment, you clearly need to ensure they stay with the company long enough to give you a reasonable return. You could ask the agency for staggered payment terms to reduce the impact of the hiring fees (e.g. 20 per cent up front, 30 per cent on the start date, 40 per cent after one month and the balance after three months). Again, every little action helps improve the cash flow!

Alternatively, why not offer your own staff a 'finder's fee' bonus? If they locate and persuade top rate staff they know to join the company, a little extra is paid to them. If recruitment agency fees might cost you up to £6,000 then why not pay an incentive to your staff of £2,000 or more per candidate? You will be saving money; and the chance of earning more should generate a strong long-term buy-in to the success of the business.

Turning to the income side, you must take every measure to ensure sales invoices are paid promptly. This is a trap many small companies fall into; believing that once a sale is made the cash is magically transferred to their bank account! Between the sale and the cash collection there are many opportunities for the unscrupulous customer to find reasons to delay payment – and every one hits your cash flow.

If possible, and appropriate to your business practices, ensure you get sufficient cash to pay for the cost of the sale, in the form of a deposit, prior to delivery. Define very clearly, and without ambiguity, the terms on which the balance of your money is to be paid. Included in this should be what the customer can expect from you in return.

Recent Market Data

In 1998, the UK government introduced the Late Payment of Commercial Debts Act. This allows firms with under 50 employees to claim interest on overdue invoices from large companies at 8 per cent above the Bank of England base rate.

Figures from the Federation of Small Businesses, which sponsored a study during 1999 into the payment times for invoices, indicates that the legislation is having little or no impact. The average time for payment of commercial invoices by PLCs in 1999 remained the same as the previous year, 46 days. However, the range of average days outstanding is startling; ranging from seven to more than 200!

Of the more than 3,000 PLCs which gave details, 20 per cent took more than 60 days to pay and 1.5 per cent over 200 days. Not surprising then that Dun & Bradstreet, one of the UK's leading business information providers, estimate that more than 40,000 companies each year fail due to payment delays.

The difficulty most small companies have is standing up to

their large clients. It takes courage to upset major customers and it can prove expensive to use the law to resolve matters. The best advice is to put in place tight credit control procedures and establish payment terms from the outset (see Chapter 6). Also, run some basic checks on new clients, using credit reference agencies or your bank, to uncover County Court judgements. The small up-front cost is a worthwhile investment.

Cash flow management: example

Mr James is a builder erecting conservatories onto residential homes. Following good business practice, he asks the householders for a deposit of 30 per cent with order. He explains that within two weeks the homeowner can expect the foundations to have been dug, the concrete base to have been laid and the dwarf walls to have been built. At this point a further 30 per cent must be paid. He has now covered his costs for the whole project! Once the conservatory is fully built, a further 30 per cent will become due. The final balance, of 10 per cent, must be paid within 14 days of completion, giving the customer time to indicate any outstanding snags. Here again, the builder will have noted what does, and does not, fall within the scope of a 'snag list'.

This example of Mr James shows how to maximise cash flow efficiency. It avoids the alternative where no payment is received until the work is completed, leaving the customer to find endless reasons not to pay. Mr James' approach also increases his company's ability to service new customers, as it reduces the burden of cash flow management.

Cash Summary

As part of your weekly reports, produce a cash summary indicating:

- Opening balance from previous report
- Movements this week (salaries, supplier payments, cash receipts etc.)
- Closing balance this report
- Expected movements for the next eight weeks.

Ideally the report should be phased by week in the form of a cash flow spreadsheet. The report should become an essential part of your weekly routine in an attempt to optimise the net inflow of cash. It might make the difference to staying in business!

Cash flow is everything checklist

1 Do not rely solely on an income and expenditure model to determine the cash requirements for the business. Take the next step and produce a cash flow forecast as well.

2 The golden rule during the first year of trading is that up to twice the income and expenditure trade gap will be required in cash.

3 Be realistic in determining the assumptions for how the business will trade. Do not kid yourself by phasing receipts or payments simply to make the model look more attractive.

4 Make a determined effort to keep your eye on the cash position. When you have other more pressing issues to deal with, such as customer queries and new sales, it is very easy to leave cash flow to your accountant or bookkeeper.

5 Deal with cash flow proactively. Check your cash balance every day and ensure there are no unusual movements on the horizon.

6 Be creative in the ways you try to optimise your cash flow. Put reasonable delays on the outflow and press hard on pre-agreed deadlines for cash inflow.

7 Always keep an up-to-date cash flow forecast for the next two months and have it checked at least once per week. It may save your business!

8 PLC's take 46 days on average to settle the invoices of small companies.

9 Where appropriate, ask for deposit from your customer sufficient to cover your exposure.

6 Daily procedures

Daily procedures are those activities that support the running of your company. They ensure that supplier bills get paid on time, staff receive their salary cheques and sales invoices get raised. Ideally they should operate whether or not a certain individual is present in the office.

It is best to identify as many of the daily procedures as possible before you start trading in earnest. As well as describing the responsibilities of employees, the procedures should also indicate what form of paperwork needs to be generated for you, the owner, to properly audit the trading activities of the business when you are not there. Even if you intend being around the company every day, start with the end in mind – when you might not be – and consider the procedures you will need then.

There are four main areas that should be considered in relation to procedures. These concern customers, suppliers, finance and staff (see Figure 1). However, the key phrase to remember in all of them is: 'If you manage the downside the upside will manage itself'.

What does this imply? Think of a worst case scenario and try to ensure that this situation can be managed successfully using your procedures (e.g. you are on holiday or on extended business away from the office, and an irate customer demands urgent attention):

- Who will take responsibility?
- What scope will that person have to satisfy the customer?
- When will the problem be escalated to the next person (in an hour, a day or a week) and what can be agreed with the customer?

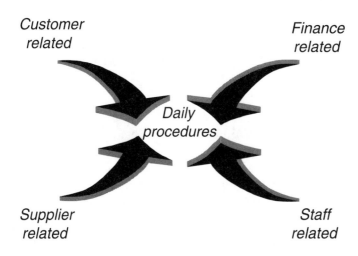

Figure 1 The four main areas of daily procedures

Daily procedures: example

I know of a retail chain in the UK that has recently introduced a home delivery service over the Internet. Eager to
try, I placed an order using the online screen and waited for
the delivery at the allotted time. As expected, some items
were not available. Some substitutions had also been made,
but the procedures here were explained by the delivery
driver who suggested I contact the local store. The customer
service was excellent. The person at the store agreed to
cancel the delivery charge and made no fuss over the
wrongly delivered items. 'We'll collect them when we deliver
your next order'.

Even in the simple example of the online order, managing
the downside (ensuring the customer remained satisfied) left
the upside to manage itself (repeat business assured). By
managing what could have been a very negative situation in a

positive and well disciplined manner, the firm ensured that I, the customer, was left feeling very satisfied. I was also made to feel confident of placing further orders in the future.

Putting more zest into your procedures

In business, few people like to endure heavily regimented daily routines – some people start their own companies to avoid them! So while introducing order in your company, make sure you do it with energy, drive and enthusiasm. Remember the PACIFY rules that should apply to every procedure you introduce:

- *People-orientated*: procedures should not cramp the style of your most important asset; your people
- *Accountable*: procedures need to hold certain people responsible for their actions. Staff need to know what is expected of them
- *Clearly understood*: procedures need to be written in plain English to avoid any misunderstanding
- *Integrated with other procedures*: make sure that some procedures do not conflict with others!
- *Fun*: the more fun is attached to the daily work environment, the greater your chance of success
- *Yearly reviewed*: make sure all your procedures are reviewed and updated (in light of the business development) at least once per year.

The reporting procedures required to make a business truly buzz will include historic data, but will also be forward looking. You will need retrospective information indicating what has happened in the last week, month or year – particularly where this relates to staff or financial matters.

The report production should be as automated as possible and not dependent upon any one person or activity. But don't assume the information is accurate just because it was printed on a computer! You can avoid becoming complacent by applying the first and second golden rules of leadership:

- Always distrust the management information
- The one thing you can always be sure of is that people will let you down.

It is not that people are necessarily trying to mislead, but everyone is human and makes mistakes and sometimes these can be hidden in the guise of a well presented management report. So be prepared to challenge the information, in a constructive and meaningful manner, to ensure the accuracy of the data you use.

Forward looking information is essential. This naturally applies to the financial data (weekly cash flow forecasts, income and expenditure analysis), but also relates to customer reports (expected future orders). As with the historic reporting, be prepared to question the figures to be sure they concur with your view of the business. If the prediction is for orders to tail off in two months' time, call up some customers and see if something has happened of which you are not aware.

Customer-related procedures

As the name suggests, these are the procedures to keep tabs on the activities surrounding one of your most vital assets – your customers! If you were not physically in the office for a period of time, how would you know that your clients were being well treated?

Customer reporting

Serving your customer needs has to be the number one activity. So you will need to review the sales income and product mix by customer (both for this week and year to date), highlighting the progress you have made in securing new business. Ensure you report:

- customer details
- products purchased this week and year to date
- sales this week and YTD as values and percentage of the total sales
- sales this time last year
- expected sales pipeline for next quarter and next year
- date of first sale
- date of most recent sale
- any other comments.

New enquiries

Produce a report showing a list of the new enquiries received during the last week from potential customers. This will give you a chance to calculate the conversion rate of enquiries to sales; it will, where appropriate, also give you a chance to see which type of marketing has been working to your best advantage. Ensure you report:

- details of the enquiry
- date/time of the call
- existing customer or new enquiry
- person spoken to/left details of enquiry with
- products interested in
- information to be sent
- how enquirer heard of us (e.g. *Yellow Pages*, word of mouth)
- next actions.

It is important to monitor how potential customers get to hear of you and which products they are interested in as it will assist in determining the effectiveness of your marketing efforts.

Terms of business

It is essential that you issue all customers with a written set of your terms and conditions of business prior to making supplies. You can ask your legal adviser for a standard set of these which might be tailored to meet your specific business needs. They should include:

- the prices you will charge for your products and services and how any discounts will be calculated
- the payment terms that will apply
- what credit checks you might run on the company if this is a new account
- number of days allowed before payment of invoice is due
- what happens if there is a late payment by the customer (e.g. interest charged on the outstanding amounts, you retain title to the goods until paid, future deliveries cease etc.)
- how you will deliver the goods and services (e.g. by courier) and if there are additional charges for this passed onto the customer
- what you will do if forces outside your control mean a delivery is delayed or damaged.

Support calls

You should monitor customer queries, the actions taken to rectify these and the amount of time they are outstanding. This form of reporting gives you the golden opportunity to contact customers and discuss any recurring problems they have faced in recent weeks.

The information gleaned from support calls analysis will show you are in touch with the issues that are affecting your customers. You can indicate how you will improve matters in the future and, as we will discuss later when considering sales technique (see Chapter 8), use this approach to separate you from the competition. Ensure you report:

- customer details
- date/time of the call
- details of the call
- current status (e.g. awaiting part, in workshop etc.)

- call now passed to...
- expected fix date
- lessons learned.

Order and delivery queries

The example of the online home shopping service above illustrates the importance of handling customer order and delivery queries efficiently. Those taking the calls need to have a clear understanding of what they can and cannot do to satisfy the customer. In these situations, a little flexibility goes a long way.

Agreeing to waive a £10 delivery charge may be an irritation, especially if the problem lies with your courier, but if it secures a future order flow worth many thousands then it is no contest. You can always argue separately with the delivery company. The important factors to note are:

- speed (problem resolved quickly and efficiently)
- service (matter handled without fuss and in keeping with their needs)
- satisfaction (the customer feels satisfied with the outcome).

Prompt resolution of customer order and delivery queries usually results in similar promptness for invoice payment.

Supplier-related procedures

Purchasing analysis

A printed list of every supplier order placed (daily or weekly), by whom and with whose authority is essential if you are to keep control of where money is being spent. It is good practice to enforce authorisation for purchases above a certain level for specified suppliers. Always list the following information:

- supplier details

- date of order
- order number
- transaction details
- full value of order
- discount received
- authorised by...
- reason for purchase (e.g. customer order, stock etc.).

Purchasing rules

Take responsibility for the initial negotiation of terms and conditions with suppliers yourself. This will ensure that the opportunity for any misunderstanding of the way you want to trade is minimised. Define the maximum limit on supplier order values over which you, or another director, must be a signatory.

Denote how, when and by whom orders may be placed (e.g. for cash with order you demand a 2 per cent discount, otherwise you expect 30 days' credit).

Faulty goods

A report showing the products that have been returned by customers as faulty will provide an insight into the performance of your suppliers. Use this to demand something; either better products, better prices and/or compensation. Detailed reporting should include:

- supplier details
- product details
- date of return by customer
- date of repair/replacement by supplier
- problems identified
- compensation offered.

Quality analysis

Have a weekly report produced showing the quality of the products manufactured, software developed or goods purchased depending upon the sector you trade in. This will give you the opportunity closely to monitor your suppliers and take appropriate action without delay where required.

Finance-related procedures

Reporting

As far as the financial reports are concerned, as a minimum each month you should have sight of a set of the following management information:

- a monthly income and expenditure forecast
- a list of outstanding debtors and creditors (including the age of debts)
- those clients approaching their credit limit and those which are overdue against payment terms
- the major income and expenditure expected during the next eight weeks (including VAT and tax payments) as part of a full cash flow forecast.

Discount rules and analysis

You should make it clear who can, and who cannot, give discounts to customers and under what terms and conditions. State when your agreement, or that of another director, is necessary.

Create a weekly report listing customer discounts given. The information should include:

- customer details
- date of transaction
- transaction details
- discount amount and reasons
- authorised by....

Staff-related procedures

Recruitment rules

A set of procedures for the hiring of new, and the firing of existing, staff is mandatory and it is worthwhile preparing standard contract terms and conditions for all members of staff. While for a small company this may seem an unnecessary cost, it will pay future dividends in case of employee disputes and in the speedy take-on of new staff.

Consult a local firm of solicitors and ask them to provide you with a copy of standard employment terms for your particular business, taking into account any special needs you might have (e.g. copyright and intellectual property ownership, payments for overtime, statutory sickness and maternity pay, notice periods, dismissal offences etc.).

Performance

It used to be that you could hire and fire staff almost at will and personal career development was something only the largest companies considered. Today's business world is different. Legislation, much of it emanating from Europe, means you now must pay much closer attention to the needs of your staff.

It is essential that each employee has a clear understanding of what is required of them. The basic details, such as hours of work etc., will be covered by their terms of employment; but the less well-defined areas, such as present and future responsibilities, career path and personal goals and aspirations should also be recorded and monitored.

It costs a great deal of time, effort and money to take on one new member of staff – even more when you include the time taken to teach them the internal procedures. So it is worth trying to hold onto your valuable asset.

Too often, small companies give up on people because of

irritating habits or perceived weaknesses. But isn't it worth discussing these with the person in an attempt to rectify matters? It could be that a training course or a change in working pattern would provide a quick fix. In any event, far better to find a way forward than throw away your sizeable investment.

Incentives

Employees used to measure their status by pay and position. However, with flattened management structures removing the career ladder and pay packages becoming more complex, incentives now play a far greater part in staff retention. Incentives are not just about bonus payments for achieving certain targets. They can also include:

- share options, where there is a chance the company may be floated onto one of the leading stock markets, such as the Alternative Investment Market (AIM) or the London Stock Exchange (LSE)
- increased annual holidays
- pension plans
- car schemes (becoming less tax efficient to the recipient due to recent legislative changes in UK)
- provision of services (such as mobile phones, telephone lines at home, subscriptions to TV packages)
- life assurance (including critical illness and death in service benefits)
- medical cover (sometimes including the employees partner and family).

Depending upon the person's age and lifestyle, it is not uncommon to find staff who consider the 'soft benefits' (e.g. number of days' holiday) as important as the 'hard benefits' (e.g. salary and cash incentives). So you might consider offering someone an 'incentives' rise rather than an annual 'pay' rise. This might consist of x per cent in additional pay and y extra days' holiday.

Finally, consider the person's tax position. If possible, and appropriate, offer the incentives in a tax paid format, to make them even more attractive.

Daily procedures checklist

1 Procedures are essential for the business from the first day of trading. They should meet the day-to-day operational requirements for smooth running and include the production of historic and forward-thinking reports.
2 Make sure the report production is automated and not dependent upon a single person or activity.
3 The key phrase with procedures is: manage the downside and the upside will manage itself.
4 Have procedures relating to suppliers, customers, finance matters and staff.
5 Make sure the procedures pass the PACIFY rules, namely:

- people-orientated
- accountable
- clearly understood
- integrated with other procedures
- fun
- yearly reviewed.

6 Ensure you get a detailed set of management reports each month with which to run the business.
7 The first golden rule of leadership is: always distrust the management information. The second is: the one thing you can always be sure of is that people will let you down.
8 Personally lay down the terms on which orders can be placed with suppliers and discounts given to customers – including who has the authority and for what amounts.
9 Work hard to find and retain good staff. Consider soft incentives for employees, not just hard.

7 Negotiating with customers and suppliers

The art of negotiation with suppliers and customers is something that has to be mastered if you are to get the most from your business venture. Those extra few percentage points that are won or lost during the cut and thrust of a sale will make all the difference at the end of the financial year.

There has been a lot written on the subject of negotiation. This chapter covers the key points that will be relevant to you, trading within the small business community, and are essential to keep your margins high. You should never be afraid of negotiation. See it as merely an essential part of every business transaction you enter into. Remember: 'If you can't negotiate, you shouldn't be in business'.

In his book, *Everything is Negotiable*! Gavin Kennedy suggests there are four types of animal behaviour in negotiation: sheep, donkey, fox or owl. The sheep is easily led towards the choices made by others. The donkey is blissfully unaware of what is possible and has the capacity for knee-jerk reactions. The fox is cunning and knows what is going on and truly believes it gets what it negotiates. Finally, the owl is wise and wants long-term relations and does not usually exploit sheep, donkeys or foxes. But beware, many owls are closet foxes!

So what are the factors that will ensure you concede a little less and gain a little more both with your suppliers and customers? Figure 1 provides some suggestions.

Everything is negotiable

Whenever you are negotiating to buy or sell, remember everything is negotiable. This means not just the price of the

Figure 1 Elements of good negotiation

products and/or services you are buying or selling but also the delivery dates and drop points, the commercial and payment terms, the warranty period, the call-out charges, etc. It is remarkable, when you are buying, how many concessions you can score with the non-price components of a transaction. Many suppliers seem to focus on the price of the deal and use this as the key determinant of whether they have got what they wanted. Well, let them go for the 'price is everything' approach. You take the route of 'don't change the price, change the package'.

Using this approach when selling, you can trade certain items that will not cost you too much but which are of significance to the buyer. You might agree to hold the products in stock for six weeks while the customer refurbishes their warehouse and then arrange delivery of the goods on a Saturday. This will cost you very little, but could assist the customer greatly.

Another time to change the package and not the price is

when you are told by a would-be buyer 'I like your proposal, but it is £5,000 more than my budget'. Everyone is tempted to rush into 'chipping' the price but that would be the wrong signal. The key phrase to note here is 'I like your proposal'. The right approach is to make a new proposal that changes the package (and the price) in order that it does fall within the buyer's budget. You will soon find out if the budget ceiling is real or just a negotiating ploy!

Aim for a win/win

There are many negotiators who believe that negotiating is all about them getting the concessions they want while the other party crumbles. Certainly you want to do the best for your own company; but if you demand so many extras from the would-be supplier that they are not sure whether the business is really worth undertaking, you will have a dissatisfied supplier and may end up with poor service.

The results of this approach can be considerable. If they do not meet the supply terms you agree with them, you could always sue for breach of contract. But what advantage does that give you? Not a great deal. You might gain financially if you follow through with the legal approach but the supplier will be much more wary the next time.

When selling, the same rules apply. You can insist that the contract terms are strictly X, Y and Z and these are definitely non-negotiable. But beware. Being too dogmatic and not being prepared to concede a few points in return for others, when these might be the ones the prospect is most sensitive about, can be a risky approach.

Every concession must be met in kind

Whether selling or buying, you must never concede a change to your proposals without receiving a corresponding concession from the other side. If you give up something for nothing the other side will simply seize it and look for the next thing! Once you have given it up you cannot easily claim credit for it later.

You must never give up anything in isolation during a negotiation. A classic example of giving something up is to offer an initial concession just to get matters under way – a taster to break the ice. *Wrong*. All this will do is encourage the other side to let you give away more without offering anything back in return! Remember: 'Negotiating means *trading* concessions that lead to a better deal for both sides'.

It is strongly recommend that concessions are always met in kind. A good forward-thinking negotiator will always look to adjust the terms of the deal so that they are better for both sides; whereas the traditional haggler is usually only interested in satisfying their own needs.

In today's complex business world, where it is increasingly difficult to separate products and services but information is becoming easier to obtain, the personal skill of negotiation has become much more important. If you can demonstrate a fair and reasonable approach to doing business in which you are aiming to find the win/win solution every time, this will score you points over the hard-nosed competitor every time.

Do not think of this approach as being the soft option; far from it! It takes real skill to think not just of your own needs but also those of others. You can still hold out and be tough on the terms that are essential to meet your own business needs, while being empathetic to the requirements of your opposite number.

To help you in your negotiations, make sure you compile a list, prior to the discussions, of the non-price variables you might trade. Ideally, these will be those items that are of low cost to you but valuable to those with whom you are negotiating. Examples of non-price variables you can trade are:

- The delivery charges. Agree to X and we will reduce the delivery charges by 50 per cent.
- The payment terms. Agree to Y and we can give you a further seven days to pay.
- The installation and set-up costs on site. If you can give us an order before the end of the week, we can keep the charges for installation and set-up at last year's rates/10 per cent off current rates, etc.
- The number of days training included in the package price. If you can agree to Y and sign up before the end of the month we can include a further Z days training free of charge.

Be a skilled negotiator

Being tough in the negotiations does not mean adopting a John Wayne posture and continually threatening your counterpart! That style of negotiation will get you nowhere – except less share of business than you might otherwise have won. Remember negotiation is all about win/win. To be a really tough negotiator you must be an *effective* negotiator – one who is able to get as much as possible for both sides. Anyone can be a tough negotiator, but it takes skill to be an effective one!

Be an effective negotiator: being an effective negotiator means not giving in to the wishes of the other side at every opportunity. Large company buyers, who are trained to get the most for themselves, will hold their ground and keep chipping away for more concessions on your part. This is particularly true where you are one of many potential vendors that they can approach as a source of supply.

They will always claim: 'Your price is too high'; 'You must do better than that'; 'Your delivery lead-times are unacceptable'; etc. To overcome these objections, always have some phrases or responses at the ready and try to raise the perceived value of what you are offering by reminding them of their own demands. A standard reply might be: 'You have stated that quality cannot be compromised. We understand this approach. We only supply the highest quality components which, independent tests have shown, last around twice as long as those of our competitors and yet we are only 25 per cent more expensive'.

Don't be a price crumbler: continuing on from the effective negotiator stance, it is essential to defend the price you have quoted. Buyers' first reactions to any proposal will be to chip away at the price. You must defend the price you have given by persuading them of the non-price related attributes your company is proposing, and that these more than justify the price you have quoted.

A buyer with time on their hands: example

I found myself leading a negotiation team for a large and strategically important piece of business that meant we had to make several visits to the head office of the prospect. The premises were lavishly ornate. Each time we met, we were kept waiting for 15 minutes or more, during which time we were left to wallow in the comfort of the sumptuous surroundings. By the time the opposing team arrived, our resolve had certainly been softened!

One of their team was responsible for giving us a very hard time and she would beat out as many concessions as possible early on in the discussions. During the first four meetings we attended, she threatened several times to end the negotiations and go elsewhere if we did not concede on certain key points. We defended bravely in the face of such extreme pressure. But importantly, her sole responsibility in life was to prise the most out of her major suppliers; she was perfectly positioned to set the scene and leave the close to her counterparts. A great team effort.

But if you subsequently have to concede something, never give it away without getting something in return (see above). Always trade any concession, particularly a concession on price. Remember the rule – don't change the price, change the package.

Try to find out the workload of the buyer: a buyer is more likely to settle with you if they are very busy. Clearly if the buyer is in a slack time, or their only area of responsibility is for negotiations and hence they have as much time as needed, you will be in for a more difficult ride.

You can use the tactics given in the example to good effect if you are in the buying role. If you are selling, you need to make every effort to plan your campaigns so that buyers have less time to indulge themselves in the niceties of negotiation. Your aim should be to keep them on the route of making a decision.

Know what your limits are

One important aspect to any negotiation is being clear how much room you have to negotiate. Before starting a negotiation, if you are selling, know what the lowest price and terms you are prepared to accept are; if you are buying, know what the highest is you will pay.

On the surface, this is obvious. But when, during the heat of negotiation, you are put on the spot to accept a particular offer you may not have sufficient time to calculate whether the revised offer gives you enough margin on the deal.

It is important that you ask for a time-out during the discussions. Ask your opposite number for a 15-minute break while you: call the office to check the up-coming delivery profile; call a supplier to check lead times; check on the up-to-date pricing with your colleagues. *Anything* that gives you time to think through the current position of the negotiation and check you are still on course.

Rules of engagement

The worst mistake to make in any negotiation is to agree with the other side too quickly, as this undermines the self-respect of both sides and their confidence in the deal. The buyer thinks they have not pushed hard enough to gain concessions. The seller is left thinking they could have placed a much higher value on the package!

Try not to go first – whether buying or selling, let the other person start the negotiations. This allows you time to determine how the other party sees the make-up of the deal and whether this is close to your perception of matters. Taking into consideration what has been noted above, make sure you do not:

- accept the deal too quickly if they make a fantastic offer
- give up any concessions unless they give up something in return.

Pre-planning is the art of preparing how you will execute negotiations. You must do this if you are to get the most from every meeting you have with your prospects, as it is no good going into negotiations simply hoping that you might get X and Y. You *must* construct a full plan of action showing what you will do in different circumstances and at what point you will call matters a day and end the discussions.

If, in advance, you are not sure of your best outcome for a negotiation meeting, do not hold it!

Stage management

When buying, a useful weapon in the armoury of the effective negotiator is stage management. This is where, for example, you deliberately set up the would-be seller by having someone interrupt you at an appropriate time during the negotiations, meaning you must immediately leave the office.

It just so happens that you accidentally (!?) leave on your desk a letter from the seller's main competitor. The salesperson cannot help themselves! They have to look at the prices being quoted and before you can say 'appliance of science', they are ready to trade at those levels rather than the higher ones they proposed.

By the same token, always be cynical with information you accidentally overhear or see. Even an office junior or the secretary can be in the negotiating team – how do you know that the buyer/seller and his/her assistant are not really wife/husband?

Think big with care

As a small business, it is very easy to be overawed by the size of some of your potential customers. Particularly during the first 18 months of trading, unusually large orders from single customers are not always good news. Why?

- During the pre-sale negotiations, you will be expected to invest a much larger amount of effort than with smaller prospects simply to keep in the discussions. This will manifest itself through several rounds of meetings, proposals, presentations and negotiation sessions. All of these activities have a direct cost to your company. But they also have an indirect cost as you are unable to go looking for other more likely candidates and you have less time to spend with your existing customers. Fine, there may be a high pay-off should you win. But before you even consider the upside, look at what it might cost you to take part in the race.
- When bidding for larger pieces of business, you will almost certainly find a consultant or expert making recommenda-

tions to the board of directors. Consultants generally make rock-solid recommendations as it is their neck on the line should there be problems after the event. Hence, you are likely to be excluded by the size of your business unit alone. To continue in the race, you must carefully consider how you will support such a large piece of business should you win it, and have concrete evidence to back up your claims to the client and their advisers.

- Should you go the whole way and win the business, your problems are just beginning! The increased time you will need to spend with the new large customer leaves less for your existing clients and may make you more dependent on one major account.

While the temptation is to give a large client everything they want (as they are the gravy train you have been looking to board), set the rules down early so you are not pulled every which way by many and varied departments. Treat them, where possible, in a similar way to your existing clients. If you do not have the staff to support this customer directly then be prepared to offload some work to an established third party that can provide similar services on a subcontract basis to you. Do this by entering into a legally binding business partnership with them.

Business partnerships provide an ideal mechanism for you to keep control of the relationship with the client without becoming too financially stretched. This approach will keep your customer satisfied. It will also be a lot less expensive than hiring an army of new staff that must be trained in your practices and products.

All of this said, there is no greater feeling than winning a large piece of business, having fought against all the odds. It takes a lot of nerve, professional handling of all the negotiations (with the client and their consultants) and great negotiation skills to win the day. You will surely have all of your powers of persuasion put to the test.

Is it worth all of the effort? Of course, but there must be a balance. During the first 18 months of trading, given all of the internal issues you must face, it is unlikely that such orders will be of significance to your company. It might therefore be best to avoid chasing after them. While every business is different and there are no hard and fast rules, you will need sufficient time to:

- put in place the essential internal procedures that are the lifeblood of the company
- become confident that you and your staff can generate sales leads
- close enough new business with smaller companies to meet overheads
- supply your customers in a coherent and confident manner.

The right time to consider the bigger fish would seem once the Foundation Circle has been well and truly established (see Chapter 2).

Negotiating with customers and suppliers checklist

1 If you can't negotiate you shouldn't be in business!

2 Everything is negotiable – so remember to use non-price variables as well. These include delivery and payment terms, number of included training and set-up days, etc.

3 The golden rule is: don't change the price, change the package.

4 Aim at a win/win result – i.e. ensure both sides progress during the negotiations. Try to avoid one-sided deals; they usually end in tears!

5 Negotiating means trading concessions that lead to a better deal for both sides.

6 Be tough but skilled in negotiations – stand your ground and don't give in too quickly. Don't be a price crumbler.

7 Try to find out the workload of the buyer. Beware if they have no other responsibilities or if they are unusually quiet at this time!

8 Know what your limits for the deal are and be prepared to walk away.

9 Pre-plan all negotiations – if they are not going to plan, call a time-out and regroup your thoughts.

10 Stage-manage, if possible, to get what you want.

11 Think big business with care – try to avoid especially large contracts during the first 18 months of trading.

8   Everything should be sales driven

You can only pay the salaries of your staff, meet the rent demands of the landlord and buy stock if you are successful at selling. A pretty fundamental statement? Well, it is not as obvious as you might imagine.

There are still too many company directors who seem to treat the sales drive of the company as a black art – or even black magic! They often consider it unprofessional to pursue a potential or existing customer with the view of selling a new product or service to them. Sales should just happen! They feel that eventually someone will pick up the telephone or call into their shop and that they should not need to chase prospects. What a fatalistic approach!

Thankfully, the days of kick the door in, hard-nosed, brash, cold-calling sales techniques are almost dead and buried. To succeed today, you must properly manage the whole sales process. The sales professional of today needs to be just that – professional. In every walk of life, people are becoming more demanding about the manner in which they are treated before, during or after a sale, and there is no longer room to take chances where customers are concerned.

Hence, you must put your sales techniques in the spotlight and ensure that you are maximising your chances of getting the business you want.

Sales as an art

Selling is an art and a science rolled into one. It is an art because it requires the person who sells to possess and use the highest possible people skills in the differing situations they come across. One day you may be dealing with a straight-talking, know what they want commercial director who insists on keeping the meetings short and to the point but demands concessions on price at every turn; the next day with the quietly spoken proprietor who demands lots of their time, respect and careful handling while expecting to be convinced she is spending her company's money wisely.

One phrase sums up the artistic side of sales: 'People buy people first, service second and the product third'.

In other words, you can have the best product on the street but, if you do not know how to sell it effectively, you will never beat the inferior brand around the corner.

People don't always buy the best product. Sometimes they do not have all of the facts to hand and so they will choose the product that has been demonstrated best to meet their needs. Also, many purchases are made on impulse. In this situation the careful handling of the selling process by an experienced sales professional, able to spot the signals made by the potential customer so as to move them from a position of browsing to buying, is essential.

The after-sales service part of your offering is also important. If you can demonstrate a truly superior service this will greatly increase your chances of making the sale. You can do this by: outlining how you handle customer queries; detailing the support you give after the sale has been made; and providing satisfied clients with whom to speak.

Sales as a science

So much for the people-related skills. What about the science of selling? There are far more attributes to selling than lots of lunches, dinners and days on the golf course with potential clients! It requires careful planning. An overall strategy, combined with well-defined tactics of what to do in different situations, usually ensures that you close more sales than you lose.

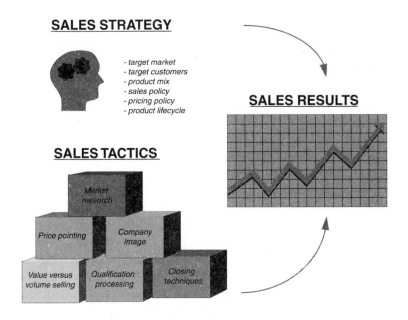

Figure 1 Approach to selling

The science of selling has been well documented in many other books, but there are some key aspects that are worthy of note to the small business owner.

Figure 1 indicates some of the components of sales strategy and tactics.

Sales strategy is long-term in nature and generally associated with the broad objectives for the business. It is not a specific set of targets or goals; rather it includes attributes of your approach to selling.

By contrast tactics generally focus on the short-term and are the means by which you will deliver the sales strategy. These are likely to become ingrained within the daily procedures of your business.

Delivering the sales results

So much for theory, how does the practical application of sales strategy and tactics deliver results?

Target customers and markets

The most important initial step is to determine those customers and markets which will be the focus of your sales activities. By segmenting customers who have similar characteristics into groups, you will be able to determine more readily in which order you should target them.

For example, if you are a high street retailer selling clothing, then you must first of all determine which sector of the market you are aiming to sell to (e.g. children, teenagers, young mothers, working people, retired people etc.). You also must check for special needs (e.g. petite, oversize, maternity wear etc.). By identifying the possible customer groups, and then choosing the sequence in which you will serve these groups, you have determined whom you will, and will not, sell to.

It is possible that some groups of customers will be either too difficult, or too expensive, to reach. It might be that you will be forced to work with certain customer groups in order to generate enough sales for the company to trade profitably. In either case, the process of identifying the potential customer groups helps you decide the right targets to give the most commercial benefit to the business.

In the fashion example above, the segmentation is quite clear. But in many other commercial sectors, the dividing line is frequently blurred and, while it may seem a trivial task from the outset to set clearly defined terms as to those you will and will not supply, the exercise can pay huge dividends in the future.

The segmentation of target markets relates to the division of business opportunities by geography or industry. If your business trades in a very small part of the country, the geographic segmentation might be very local (i.e. towns in the area). If you cover the country, the segments may be counties or even regions. The industrial segments might include manufacturing, energy, technology, etc.

It is likely that during the first year or so of trading, you will sell to only one or two market segments. This will provide time to assimilate knowledge of the segment, gain experience in the working of the market, and build some credibility and sales

Sales strategy: example

I knew of a sole trader window cleaner working for residential customers. One day, he was asked if he would be interested in subcontracting to a major commercial firm providing services to its customers. When he started up the company, he did so in a hurry. Hence, he did not have a clear sales strategy (i.e. he had not decided to stay totally with the residential sector) and the opportunity of much better paid and regular work attracted him. He decided to accept the challenge.

There were some start-up costs for the new work as he needed to buy more equipment – cradles, tackle and rope gear – not to mention revamping the insurance cover for the business.

If he had taken the time to think this through, what he would have realised was that the better rates in the commercial sector would only apply in the early months during which time he lost his residential customers. Within six months he was at the mercy of the terms offered by the main contractor, out of the house-to-house market and wishing he had considered more carefully the contractor's offer.

credentials. You can then expand into other segments. This approach keeps costs under control, while maximising the chances of sales success.

Be clear about whom you will and will not supply from the beginning and do not change course without extremely good reasons to do so. Beware if you do decide to adjust your sights without proper consideration. There may be more sinister forces at work – as the window cleaner in the strategy example found out to his peril!

Market Research

Concrete market research is essential to determine why people will buy from you rather than another company that is already supplying them. This does not necessarily have to be very expensive or time-consuming to create. In the fashion sector, competitors would include other high street retailers (nationwide as well as independents), market traders and mail order catalogues.

Remember, you will be the new kid on the block and the customers you are trying to attract will need a good reason to buy from you rather than a name they know and trust. So how will you differentiate yourself from the other suppliers?

Identify your unique selling points (USPs)

These are the characteristics that set you aside from the competition and will be the major features you will highlight. It could be that you intend to supply only the most expensive, one-off dresses to women aged approximately 25–45. Price will not be an issue. Rather the quality, exclusivity and uniqueness under the slogan 'No one else will be wearing this dress', will be the key.

Alternatively, it could be you want to sell to men on a tight budget, and so you will seek out the best quality at the keenest prices. Here price *is* the issue. Your promotional material will highlight the cost effectiveness of the products you are selling and that these clothes cannot be found at better prices anywhere else.

Products and Services

Having identified the customers and markets you intend targeting in the short-term and beyond, it is useful to fine-tune the products and services you will supply.

Timing here is important. By mapping out the products and services you intend supplying to your target customers and markets over the next three years or so, you will better be able to plan with suppliers and begin building marketing campaigns.

The life of products and services is also important. The fashion trade is driven by four distinct seasons and hence, once a season has ended, a product line is unlikely to be continued. Computer software, by comparison, has a much longer life cycle with packages often being upgraded, or new releases issued, every six to 12 months.

The product life should directly affect your investment in associated in-house activities, such as marketing and supplier negotiations. Products which are transitory or very short-term should not warrant the level of attention or activity which main-stream lines demand.

Using the axiom that people buy people first, service second and the product third, your tactics must ensure that the people who sell your product and meet your potential and existing customers, match the profile you want to project as the image of your company. It is essential that the seller learns how to match the client. Matching the client means changing the style of delivery to mirror the behaviour patterns of the would-be buyer. You need to use the first few minutes while speaking with them to understand their mannerisms (e.g. how fast they speak, how quickly they move the conversation on, any personal quirks they have, etc.).

The image of the company

Think about the image you are projecting of your company with the staff who are at the sharp end of the sale – namely those that are the first to meet the new customer. This might be the receptionist. How your switchboard is managed says a lot about the company, so why not try discreetly calling your own company from time to time posing as a potential buyer. See how you are treated and monitor how long it takes for you to be helped.

Ensure that you build an image of the company and promote it at all costs. This might be a phrase or slogan, or it could be the way you service your clients (e.g. a well-known haulage firm prides itself in having drivers that are always smartly dressed, including shirt and tie).

Ease of purchase

Many companies make the process of placing an order so complex that the customer is left not sure if they are ordering the correct goods or not! Use the KISS syndrome – keep it simple stupid!

If you have a large number of products from which the customer may choose (different colours, sizes, etc.) then at least ensure that there is a modicum of logic to the product coding sequences (e.g. 1234/GR for colour green, 1234/RE for colour red or 780/12 for size 12, 780/14 for size 14).

As for the order forms, these too need to be kept as simple as possible. One of the fatal mistakes is the quantity box – where the customer is ordering 1 × 144 envelopes and gets 144 × 144 envelopes because they put 144 in the quantity column by mistake. If the code number is structured properly this simple mistake should be avoided. But why not have two columns, one showing the units ordered and one the total quantity to be shipped?

One thing is assured. The companies that make placing an

order difficult and time-consuming will not maximise their levels of business.

Time spent with potential customers

The amount of time you or your staff intend spending with each new customer is also important. If someone is spending £500 with you and your weekly turnover is £5,000 then perhaps they are worthy of more attention – particularly if this might be a repeat order. But is it worth spending so much time with someone parting with say £50 if your weekly trade is £10,000?

Only you as the owner can determine. But sometimes, having taken account of all of your direct and indirect costs, an individual sale might end up costing you money! Better to determine from the start how new customer enquiries, support calls and complaints will be handled by devising the rules and procedures all staff should follow. These should list all of the likely cases you will meet during the course of doing business and how each situation will be tackled; everything from faulty goods, after-sales service and warranty to volume and one-off discounts (see chapter 6).

The pricing levels you choose should be linked to the target customers and markets you are chasing, the types of product you are offering and the image you are promoting for the company. The extreme positions, high price and low volume or low price and high volume, are the end points of the classical Keynesian economics demand curve which is indicated in Figure 2.

The extreme points are the most straightforward in terms of price pointing as, through relatively small amounts of market research, you can determine the competitive landscape. However, working at the extreme price points has its dangers. Price too high and you risk exposing the business to long periods between sales, which will have an impact upon the cash flow. Price too low, and there are combined pressures: custo-

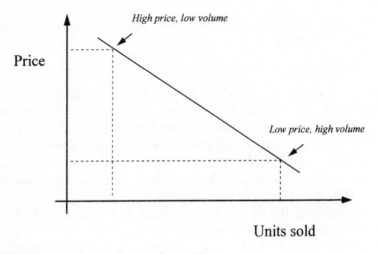

Figure 2 Keynesian economics demand curve

mers passing over the products because of perceived poor quality; and greater pressure on the internal procedures and stock management systems.

Whatever pricing policy you adopt, ensure that those selling the products and services have a very clear understanding of why you price the way you do. It could be the high quality of the product that demands a premium price. It might be that you price 10 per cent below the only other stockist in the country or that your price includes other added value benefits, such as a two year warranty.

Professional service companies

If you are in the professional services area (e.g. consultants, bespoke computer software suppliers, accountants), it is likely that you will need to meet your potential customers many times over before an order is placed. Here again, every meeting provides the opportunity to strengthen or weaken your claim to the new business. Everything depends upon:

- how you listen (you have two ears and one mouth so use them in that ratio)
- how you take the information given by the customer and relate this to the products and/or services you might offer
- how you interrelate personally.

The last point is key. Body language, posture and vocal tone are very important in ensuring empathy with the client. Avoid being too self-opinionated, arrogant or rude. Assertiveness is fine, so long as you do not cross the threshold and become overbearing.

A good move is to show you've done your homework on the company by presenting information about your potential client during the initial presentation. It does not have to be extensive. Details should include their relative position in the market, their financial strength (from audited accounts) and their major competitors, most of which is readily available either from Companies House or through the Internet – even their own web page! By showing you have taken the initiative to understand the client's business, you will have begun to separate yourself from the other potential vendors.

Finally, don't always try to win the business on price. It is rare for business to be won on price alone. If you decide to price above the competition but present a more professional approach you will probably still win the day. A genuine concern for a client's needs balanced with a realistic view on pricing, in order that you make a reasonable return on your time invested (pre-sales, design, development, delivery and post-implementation support), is not only good for long-lasting client relations, it is essential for you to stay in business. The axiom here is: 'Turnover is vanity, profit is sanity'.

The sales cycle

All selling is driven by the sales cycle. All of the points made above are part of that cycle and Figure 3 is *aide-mémoire* of the steps you must take to make that next sale.

Figure 3   The sales cycle

You should never be afraid to walk away from a potential sale if you decide it is not worth pursuing. Perhaps the prospect is only fishing for information and not committed to the project. Maybe the margins that you will make do not justify the investment the sale will require. Possibly you feel the customer requirements will take you away from your core business. Whatever the reason, make the decision as soon as possible in order to protect your reputation in the market and your own long-term aims and aspirations.

Qualification process

The qualification of a client should be the first thing you do. If you own and run a shop, this will be initiated through a few direct questions to the customer in your store. In other circumstances, such as if you are speaking on the telephone, ensure you have a 'qualification sheet' in front of you.

It is essential that the intentions of any prospect are validated very early on in the sales process. The person calling you, or walking into your shop, could be a complete time-waster. They might not be interested in placing an order for at least another year or so; they might even be doing some market research on behalf of the competition!

So always be prepared to question them hard. Pose the questions that will allow you to verify their intentions in order that you can determine how much time to spend with them.

What should you ask? Your qualification sheet should at the very least include (as appropriate):

- Their personal details (name, address, telephone number)
- How did they get to hear about you as a supplier – useful for your marketing purposes. This is an easy question to start with as it has no hidden agenda
- When do they intend to place the order?
- Approximately how much do they expect the work/product/ service to cost and/or what is their budget?
- To which other companies are they talking? This is a good indication of how seriously they are treating the exercise
- What are the very important criteria that must be met in order to win the business? Is it price alone? If so, you might want to walk away now! Are there other factors such as product quality, after-sales service, well established in the business, a local company, a member of a certain trade organisation, etc.?
- What do you need to do next? Is there a formal tender process to respond through and, if so, when is the latest date for submission? Who will make the final decision as to which supplier has won the order and how will you be informed? Will you need to make any formal presentations and if so when and where?

Qualification is intended to assist you in deciding if this is business you want to pursue. Not all business is good business. Never be afraid to walk away from certain types of work; this is particularly true if the margin is tight or if the order:

- requires lots of your time for relatively little reward
- is complex in nature and might distract you from winning other business
- is high risk and could end in failure
- may damage your reputation in the general market – bad news always travels faster than good
- may take you away from those areas of business activity in which you have a strength (as we defined in the overall strategy); if it is outside an area in which you can perform professionally, reject the opportunity.

The qualification process does not end if, and when, the prospect passes the first test. Throughout the whole sales cycle, ensure you carefully validate the answers given by the prospect and systematically requalify at every opportunity to be sure they are not wasting your time.

What about the competition?

A couple of final points of note to improve the amount of business you win. Arrange for someone you know to call your competition from time to time to see how they price goods and promote their business. Get them to comment on other suppliers. It is a good way to see how you are perceived in the market and whether the competition is playing professionally or not (i.e. are they just trying to blacken your name?).

It is unprofessional to knock the competition. Everybody needs choice and the people you compete against are helping to make the business world a more competitive and healthy environment! If you make a habit of just trying to put down your competitors, the chances are your potential client will not listen and simply put their business elsewhere.

Closing the sale

Perhaps the most important aspect of the whole of the sales process is the close. You can present yourself in the best light possible, do the most prolific and entertaining presentations, but you must be able to close the sale.

The close of a sale is not a one-time activity. You should ideally attempt several closes with the potential customer throughout the sales cycle to see the reaction you receive. Why?

It keeps the process moving forward and saves time. It also draws out objections from the customer, essential if you are to

Closing the sale: example

I had a particular prospect that I initially spoke to on the telephone. Using the qualification process, I was convinced that this would be an ideal customer for my business. The prospect had a reasonable chain of stores, knew what he wanted from the supplier and expected to have the benefits clearly identified before making any decisions.

During the next 18 months (yes, that is right, 18 months), I chased the prospect on a regular basis providing the information he requested and attempting many times to close the business. Every time further objections were forthcoming. Eventually, during the final negotiation meeting at the prospect's office, it became clear that his stalling tactics were to check my persistence to the task and the stamina I had shown scored highly.

The prospect did indeed become a good customer, an excellent reference site and helped secure many new clients thereafter.

keep the sales cycle moving. But remember, a *no* is not necessarily the end of the sale! Never give up, as the client may still be prepared to buy at a later date.

What kind of closes are there? There are hundreds, but here are four techniques that outline the type of approach you should take. There is no need to be too heavy with the prospect. Do not worry if they are not ready to close at the time you initially prompt, for there will be other opportunities and chances, perhaps at the next meeting.

1 *The direct close*: 'Shall we go ahead then?'; or, 'What else do we need to do to get your business?' You are directly prompting the customer to either agree to proceed or to place a further objection in your path.
2 *The summary close*: here you assume the client is ready to go ahead by summarising the key benefits and then asking for the order (e.g. 'We have agreed that our approach will enable you to reduce costs by the 10 per cent you asked for. The budget for the project is approved and our costs fall within its scope. When might we be able to start the training for your staff?')
3 *The alternative close*: this is used all the time in restaurants. 'Red or white wine Sir?' leaves you with little room to manoeuvre as you seem to be buying wine in either case. You can use a variation on this in a limitless number of ways.
4 *The final objection close*: if the prospect raises an objection that is based on a clear misunderstanding or is easy to answer you can use this as a means to close. 'Is this the only thing stopping us going ahead?'; or, 'If I can satisfy you on this point, are you ready to proceed?' Answer the objection and you are home and dry.

To win any piece of business, whether an order for £50 or £50,000, you must persuade the customer that by parting with

102

their money in exchange for your promises they will be better off than they are at present. Put yourself in their shoes. Have you totally persuaded the customer that your proposal makes commercial sense? If you were in their shoes, would you make the commitment?

If you cannot honestly answer 'yes' to these last two points then your chances of closing the sale will be greatly reduced. Belief and self-confidence, not just in your own techniques of selling but in the products and services you are proposing, far outweigh all other factors.

Being successful in improving your sales has as much to do with personal confidence, communication skills and interaction with your prospects as it has with sales techniques. All that sales techniques do is highlight the methods you should follow and ensure you do not miss any steps.

When dealing with small companies, your personal credibility counts for a great deal. If you ensure that you keep your promises, do not overstretch yourself by agreeing to commitments you cannot keep and deal honestly and professionally with clients, your sales will increase.

The role of brand and marketing

If you had to list those concepts which are most often confused in business life, it is a fair bet that brand and marketing would be high on the list.

Brand is a difficult concept to grasp. It is best described using the analogy of a brand stamped onto animals – meaning you can tell the origin of cattle or sheep simply by observing their brand. The brand identifies something unique about the bearer. Just by observing it, you are able to determine a great deal more information than simply the symbol alone.

Think of any major brand, such as BMW or Nike, and you immediately conjure up an image associated with it. See the brand logo (e.g. BMW blue and white circle or Nike tick) and you instantly recall the attributes of the brand.

It takes enormous amounts of investment to build the brand image (the qualities you associate with the brand), the brand name and the brand logo (the symbol that gives recognition of the name and the image). It is therefore not surprising that company brands are often the biggest asset on the owner's balance sheet. Global brands are only within the financial scope of the largest and most successful businesses.

Marketing, on the other hand, is available to all. It represents the process by which you promote the products and services you sell and the image you want to portray about your company. The latter point is essential. What does your company stand for? Is your name recognised in the local or national community?

Marketing need not cost a fortune, but to be effective it needs to be:

- well-targeted
- clear and concise
- consistent.

Well-targeted because it must reach the audience you are trying to influence. If this campaign is designed to promote an upcoming sale you are holding then it must quickly reach those people you are trying to attract. What are the 'hot buttons' that will tempt potential customers to the sale? Price? Brand names? A local celebrity to sign autographs? If this is a more general company promotion then the results may not be seen in the near-term and it is likely that the target audience to be reached will be much wider than for the upcoming sale.

Clear and concise because that is what marketing needs to be! Far too often, advertisements are long and complex. This runs the risk that the target audience may miss the message you are attempting to get across or, worst of all, simply ignore it!

Consistent because regular marketing is a way of building and supporting a local brand. You might not create the global recognition of BMW or Nike but in your area or niche market, people will become acquainted with what your company stands for. It could be quality, speed, service or low price. Make sure the marketing supports this, as it helps to promote differentiation between your company and the competition.

The Marketing Circle

We have identified the role of brand and marketing, but what about the ways of reaching your target audience? The Marketing Circle is made up of three layers (see Figure 4). The inner layer is the target or, in marketing speak, demographic audience. It is usually defined by age, sex and/or socio-economic group. The middle layer shows the types of marketing you can use to reach the target audience. Finally, the outer layer represents the reason for the marketing – is it to promote a particular event, a range of products and services or your company's brand/image?

Brochures and direct mail represent an ideal way of promoting products and services. Depending on the value of the products it is trying to market, the brochure could range from an inexpensive one-page A5 black and white sheet to an eight-page full colour glossy document. There are companies that provide reasonably high quality finished products at low cost by putting your print run alongside many others. You normally need to order by the thousand. But prices drop even further once you get past the 10,000 mark.

Logic suggests that you should invest only in brochures that do not age over time. This can be done by avoiding copy which dates the products or services into an era (e.g. Year 2000

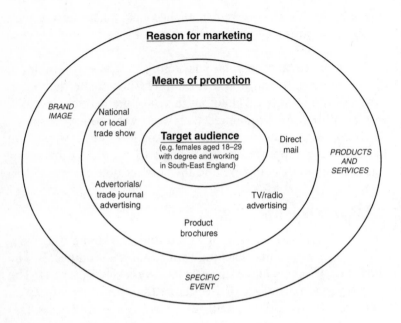

Figure 4 The Marketing Circle

conversion services). You should also consider how the brochure can be extended as you develop your products over time.

If one of your clients will agree to an article being written about their experiences of using your company, you can prepare an *advertorial*. This is where a trade journal or magazine agrees to print your editorial in return for you taking an advertisement alongside – hence (advertorial).

You might even consider going much further and producing a colour pull-out to fit within the centrefold of the journal. This would cost slightly more to produce but, at certain times of the year, some publications might be only too pleased to take such a deal. Given the large print run, you are more than likely to be left with a large stock of brochure material too!

Taking part in either a local or national trade show is a major undertaking. It requires considerable organisation to prepare for the show, takes some of your valuable sales and administration staff away from their usual duties for several weeks to prepare and attend the event and means you must take on part-time cover while the show is running. Post the event, there could be hundreds of enquiries to follow up on.

The reason for attending such shows is either to increase sales enquiries or promote your company brand/image. While such shows will usually meet these objectives, their cost to the business will always be much larger than simply the direct costs of attending.

The most effective way to approach TV/radio advertising is through an advertising agency. They will have relationships with various local broadcasters and will contract to deliver an agreed amount of viewers/listeners for a set price. Adverts are usually 30 seconds in length. Both TV and radio companies use standard measures which determine the number of people who actually watched/listened to the adverts and hence you can monitor the progress of your campaign.

You might, for example, buy a campaign with an advertising agency lasting for three months, using local radio. The commercials might be aimed at one or more audience demographics (such as men aged 18–34, women aged 16–49, people with mortgages or those looking for work) and there would be an agreed delivery schedule in terms of the number of people reached.

The advertising agency should be able to assist in all aspects of the transaction, from helping with the contract negotiations with the broadcaster, to the making of the commercials and the reporting of the results. Local radio has become a very popular medium for small and medium-sized businesses. This is because it has a well-defined audience, is relatively inexpensive to advertise on and, in recent years, has seen its audience share rise form 2 per cent in 1990 to over 5 per cent in 1999.

Everything should be sales-driven checklist

1 Selling is an art and a science rolled into one.
2 The golden rule of selling is: people buy people first, service second and the product third.
3 Devise a sales strategy (long-term plan) and stick to it.
4 Know who your competitors are, sort out your own USPs and determine the market you want to compete in.
5 Devise a range of sales tactics which will deliver your overall strategy.
6 Try matching the client when building a relationship with them.
7 Build a clear image of your company and try to project this into the market.
8 Don't make it too difficult to do business with your company by putting internal obstacles in the way.
9 Calculate the right amount of time to spend with potential customers – and if it is too much then be prepared to walk away.
10 Not all business is good business – judge each sale on its relative merits.
11 Do some homework on potential clients – not just to show you know your market but also to help determine how good a customer they might be!
12 Follow the sales cycle and qualify at every step.
13 Be aware of the competition and regularly check their product offerings. Also try to find out what they are saying about *you*.
14 Learn the various closing techniques including the direct, summary, alternative and final objection closes.
15 Promote your personal self-confidence and build credibility with your clients to increase your success.
16 *Brand* and *marketing* are not the same thing.
17 Use various marketing techniques to develop your local company brand and reach the desired target audience.

9   Valuing and selling the business

Suppose that you have followed the methods described above, built your business and are now at a point where you would like to consider realising the proceeds from your hard efforts. How do you value the business and, as important, who will be the purchaser?

Small companies are notoriously difficult to value as they do not conform to the well-defined rules that are laid down for much larger private- and publicly-owned businesses. However, this chapter outlines some of the methods you might consider and indicates a number of the more important issues you should bear in mind when attempting to reach a realistic value and find a willing suitor for your company.

The value of the business

Let us start by considering the value of your business. There are several ways in which this might be determined, but it is usually derived from mathematical calculations using either net profit or sales revenue. There can be alternatives; if, for example, your company is highly dependent upon the size of the client base, a prospective buyer might wish to offer you so much per additional customer.

Each approach has its own pros and cons, but using a formula is far better than the alternative – simply taking a number out of the air!

The net profit method takes the average annual net profit your company has generated during, say, a three year period, and multiples this by a factor – the 'industry multiple'. The result is intended to indicate the amount of profit the company is likely to generate over the next few years. It clearly helps if profits are not showing a downward trend. The industry multiple is also key.

Certain industries command higher multiples than others. The smallest might be manufacturing or retail (say 4 to 8 times) with the highest being software or hi-tech (say 10 to 50 times). In the rush to buy Internet stocks at the start of 2000, some small technology companies were valued with industry multiples over 1,000!

Suppose you are a small retail shop which has been trading for four years and has the business track record shown in Figure 1. By using differing industry multiples and differing time periods, it is possible to get completely different valuations for the same business.

If we take the average net profit for any three-year period – Years 2 to 4, 3 to 5 (where Year 5 is still an estimate) or 4 to 6 (where Years 5 and 6 are estimates) – and multiply the result by the industry multiple (in this case a range from 4 to 8), we get very differing values.

As a small company proprietor, you need to be creative! It is no good considering the last three years' profit if your company has been in existence for under six years. Why? Because you

Year	actual 1	actual 2	actual 3	actual 4	estimate 5	estimate 6
Revenue	£125,000	£221,000	£265,000	£465,000	£525,000	£605,000
Net Profit	-£10,500	£12,500	£15,500	£37,500	£52,000	£62,750

Total profits years 2 - 4	£65,500	
Total profits years 3 - 5		£105,000
Total profits years 4 - 6		£152,250

Value of business using average net profit with multiple of		Yrs 2 - 4	Yrs 3 - 5	Yrs 4 - 6
	4	£87,333	£140,000	£203,000
	6	£131,000	£210,000	£304,500
	8	£174,667	£280,000	£406,000

Figure 1 Business track record

will not have had sufficient time to build a strong track record of revenue growth on which to value the company. Hence, take advantage of the forecasts you produce for the future.

In the example shown in Figure 1, even using the lowest multiple for the industry, it is possible to increase the potential value of the company from £87,333 to £203,000 simply by changing the period under consideration. As stated above, for small companies there are few hard and fast rules for valuation. Hence, if you can support your case that this is a vibrant and growing business, with great prospects yet to be realised, you are far more likely to achieve a valuation towards the top end.

Better still, go for a higher multiple. As there are few definite guidelines where small companies are concerned (other than not trying to be too greedy), propose the highest reasonable multiple possible so that you have room for manoeuvre during negotiations. Remember each extra point on the multiple is one extra year's profit that you are asking someone to pay for in advance.

If you use decide to use a revenue-based multiple rather than net profits, it is possible you might get one times annual revenue rather than, say, six times annual profits. Again, depending upon whether you use the current year or the estimate for next, values can change.

The key determinant is whether your business is driven more by the revenue or the profit it produces. A larger company might decide that it is better to buy your company for its customer base and ability to generate sales rather than its profit base, as the costs can be cut once it becomes part of a larger group.

Selling the business

So much for you valuing the business. What about finding a suitable purchaser? This will be one of the most difficult tasks you will undertake in your business life and the difficulty and heartache of the activity should not be underestimated.

There will be a number of false starts, a lot of energy spent with time-wasters and many disappointments as people under-value your company and you decide not to proceed. But keep trying! Rest assured that there is always someone out there looking for a company just like yours; it may just take time to find them!

Even once you have found a suitable buyer, be prepared for a lengthy process involving much discussion and negotiation, far more than you might have expected. It could take months to finally complete the legal aspects of a deal that was agreed over a drink in the pub!

As far as finding the likely buyer is concerned, there are several options open to you. Clearly you need to find a person or corporate body that has the resources to pay you the price you are looking to achieve. A good start point is for you to investigate local companies in your industry that are either part of a larger group or a PLC. You need to find a person that will provide you with an introduction on the inside of the target company; ideally, contact with the ultimate decision-maker.

For example, our retail shop owner might wish to contact the local manager of a large group of independent stores that trades in a similar area or sector so as to get a meeting with either the finance or managing director.

Other alternatives include similar groups with a common interest in your sector. Hence, our high-street retailer might decide to contact their local or national trade association or the Institute of Directors to get a list of those companies that trade in their sector or who have expressed an interest in purchasing other small businesses.

Every Tuesday, the *Financial Times* provides details of businesses for sale. Many thousands of would-be buyers and sellers, as well as potential brokers (i.e. those wanting to bring two willing parties together for a small percentage of the overall value of the transaction), check the paper each week for new opportunities. If you do decide to advertise,

113

ensure you use a mailbox number and be as specific as possible. You will get some unwelcome replies however well you word the advert – including those trying to offer you money to refinance the company and stay in business rather than sell.

Your accountant could also be a source of useful hints in terms of finding a suitable purchaser. Within the portfolio of companies she or he serves, it is very likely that there will be businesses expanding rapidly. A ready-made vehicle, such as yours, might reduce the capital risk or time required compared to organic growth. The beauty of this method is the introduction. You will not need to make the running as your accountant will have done the hard work for you!

Sale of Business document

Whichever route takes you to a suitable purchaser, one essential requirement is the preparation of a Sale of Business document that can be used by the purchaser to evaluate your company. This is one of the most important documents you will write. Hence, paying for some professional assistance is very worthwhile.

As an indication of what will be required, listed below are the main headings you will need to include and the sort of information that you should provide.

1 *Executive summary (1–2 pages)*: explain what the company does; how long you have been trading; your main suppliers and customers; provide a brief overview of your present and expected financial state (e.g. turnover is presently £800k rising to £1m next year and we make 15 per cent net profit); your USPs; and, most importantly, why you are selling *now* and how much you want for the business.
2 *Introduction (1–2 pages)*: provide more history of the

company including why it was formed and what your objectives were; who the current shareholders and directors are and what they will do after the sale; who you consider to be the best targets for the business; and any trends in the market.

3 *The market (2–3 pages)*: to show you understand the market and its potential, you should provide a good overview of the sort of products that are demanded and why; the key features required by potential customers; a review of differences between, say, the UK, European and US markets; and an indication of the major barriers to entry.

4 *The competition (3–4 pages)*: you should name your current competitors and their size, and outline how you see yourself in relation to them (e.g. how often you come up against them, how often you win, your USPs etc.). A section on product pricing and how sensitive the market is to price changes is also beneficial. You should also indicate the likely competition you expect from new players entering the market.

5 *Strengths, weaknesses, opportunities, threats (SWOT analysis)*: one of the simplest ways to get a complete picture of the business is to draw a SWOT chart. This has four quadrants and in each you should indicate the key points (around ten) that you consider to be important.

Appendices:

I *Key personnel*: include their ages, skills, experience, and indicate whether or not they will stay with the business post-sale.

II *Summary profit and loss*: for previous three years if possible and include your budgets/forecasts for next three (two in detail one in summary) with cash flows.

III *Current capital assets*: draw up a list of all your capital assets (and liabilities) with associated values and write-off policies.

Remember, the purpose of the document is to provide a clear picture to any would-be buyer of the state of your business – both the current and future state. However, it should be written from a positive standpoint. You cannot give false information or mislead; but you can and must provide the details so as to maximise the chances of the reader taking the opportunity further.

Due diligence

When you have agreed a deal in principle with a potential buyer, the first process they will undertake is *due diligence*. The purpose is to check that the basis of the proposed transaction is sound.

It is impossible to deliver absolute certainty. However, especially when part of the process includes making an assessment of the future value of the business, due diligence gives the buyer the chance to demand proof of the claims you have made in the Sale of Business document and during negotiations.

Due diligence should touch every part of your company activities; but do not be alarmed! The process is aimed at verifying to the best of everyone's ability that what you have said and stated is true and that there are no nasty secrets lurking. So why should you worry?

To ensure that matters do not get bogged down, the buyer should produce a checklist of the items they want to verify. This will include: customer and supplier lists with account balances; stock details; personnel records; sales prospect lists; last three years' audited and present management accounts; administrative items such as bank accounts, insurance policies, building leases etc.; intellectual property rights; pension and post-retirement benefits; and long-term contracts for cars or buildings. This is *not* the exhaustive list but it gives you an indication of the scope.

By now you might be thinking that the whole process can leave you exposed, especially if the potential buyer subsequently decides not to proceed with the purchase of your company. Absolutely correct! Hence there are two other factors strongly recommended before you let anyone close to due diligence with the business:

- Employ the services of a specialist lawyer. By this I mean a corporate legal adviser of the type that is familiar with company mergers and acquisitions
- Sign a confidentiality/non-disclosure agreement with the potential buyer before you give away any important information.

The final payment

Deciding in what form you will take payment for the business is perhaps the most important consideration. From the purchaser's side, they want to keep your interest in the company for as long as possible in order that they quickly realise their investment. They will often ask you to work as a consultant to the business post acquisition for a short period. Your role will diminish during this time.

From your viewpoint, you may want to extricate yourself in order that you can begin planning what to do next. There is, therefore, a balance to be struck by both parties.

As for how you are paid for the business, the options include:

- cash in full and you leave immediately
- some cash now with the balance paid in say six months during which time you act as a consultant
- a small portion of cash now and the balance paid in 12 months with a bonus (say up to 50 per cent more) if the company performs ahead of the targets set. This naturally implies your existing management team must remain intact

117

to give you the best chance of meeting the new owners' objectives. Two downsides are that it slows integration between companies and might result in a lower final business value if the targets are not delivered
- a split of cash and stock where the purchasing company is listed on a stock market.

Clearly there are many combinations of the above, but the key messages are flexibility and creativity to your approach. Finally, it is well worth seeking assistance on how best to utilise your allowances and minimise tax exposure. As the legislation on these matters is updated almost every year, paying for up-to-date, clear and professional advice is essential.

Valuing and selling the business checklist

1 Small companies are very difficult to value.
2 There are standard methods which can be used, including an industry standard multiple times the average profits or sales revenue for a three-year period.
3 Be realistic but positive in your outlook for valuing the business.
4 The sale process can be protracted. Don't expect instant success, even once you have a deal in principle with a would-be buyer.
5 You will need to write a Sale of Business document to assist in selling the company. It is an important part of the selling process, so employ some help.
6 The first process post-agreeing a deal will be due diligence. This may seem like a nightmare but it will avoid any bad feelings later.
7 During the sale, employ the services of a corporate lawyer and sign a confidentiality/non-disclosure agreement with the would-be purchaser.
8 The final payment for the business can be a mix of cash and shares. There may be an earn-out bonus if you and your team stay post merger.

10   Other factors

When you have sorted out all of the business angles and taken stock of the practical advice given so far, there are just the five Ps to consider! These are for you; for your health and peace of mind and hopefully the strength to see it through to the end.

P1 is Physical

If you want to survive in today's stressful and often gruelling business world, it is essential that you take time out several times per week to do some form of physical exercise.

This is not a lecture on getting fit. But you must have some form of activity that allows you to escape from the company and its pressures. Personally, I have always worked out at a gym. This allows me to release the tension that builds up during the week so that I can better focus on the issues behind the challenges rather than the challenges themselves.

I set myself tough physical targets and monitor my progress against these over time. I spend around 45 to 60 minutes per session every other day. So you can see this is a real investment. But I think it pays huge dividends.

Other people go for extended walks, play golf, swim, ride or run. Whatever form it takes, make sure you do at least half an hour every other day of physical exercise – where you push the body's heart rate well above its normal level and where you lose yourself in the activity.

There will clearly be physical benefits over time. But there are great mental benefits to be had almost immediately as you find you become more able to cope with pressure and better able to focus your mind. Keep your health in check. Get fit for business.

P2 is Personality

In the chapter on selling, it was noted how important person-ality is – people buy people first. The ability to present yourself positively, with confidence and stature but with the balance of listening twice as much as you speak, pays huge dividends in business.

I have always tried to be approachable to everyone I meet, whatever their status in business, their race, colour, age, sex or creed. Being the managing director of the company does not, in my books, mean that the person takes on superhuman status and hence deserves different treatment.

You need to have a very positive mental approach to dealing with people and to problem-solving. If you cannot get along easily with others or if you have an inability to think issues through in a clear and logical manner without becoming frustrated or irritated, you are unlikely to succeed.

As the leader of the company, your staff will see you as the guide to how they conduct their affairs with customers, suppliers and other staff. Do not give them any opportunity to misunderstand what is required. From the start direct them in the way of clear communication, based on the attitude of 'no problem is too difficult'. Every issue is really just another opportunity.

P3 is Punctuality

One of the most frustrating habits of some people in business is their inability to arrive on time for appointments. It is not only rude to those who make the effort, it is wasteful for others who probably have better things to be doing than waiting for an individual.

Many years ago, I worked in a company that was run by a well-known UK financier. His attitude to meetings was simple. If you were late for the meeting, even by as little as two minutes, you were excluded. It was no good protesting that the lift was out of order, or that you were caught on the telephone. He would retort that you should have taken account of these potential issues by taking the stairs or by not taking a call so close to the start time.

As a result, very few people were late for his meetings and you always knew what would happen if you did arrive after the event!

While I do not recommend taking such drastic measures, I would suggest you get everyone to make an effort not to be late for meetings. Sometimes it is unavoidable. If so, let everyone know that you will be late and decide if it would be better to reschedule.

As for those who come to meet you, whether customers, suppliers or staff, do not keep them waiting any longer than is necessary. It sends out the wrong message and sets a bad example.

P4 is Precision

Attention to detail is of paramount importance. To truly succeed in business you must be able to think ahead of the game and almost second-guess what type of problems lie ahead. You will be better able to do this if you regularly take time out to study the detail of your company (such as the latest management reports, the income and expenditure and cash flow forecasts) so that your understanding of their content seems innate.

One great failing is to read computer-printed reports as though they cannot be wrong! They are only as good as the information fed into them. My suggestion is to consider what underlies the figures and be prepared to ask questions such as:

● Why did the salary bill increase by 5 per cent this month when there were no pay increases?

- Why did we have such an increase in returns last month versus this time last year/last month?
- I agreed to discount company ABC's invoices by 2 per cent if they paid by 5 April – they have taken the benefit but where is the payment? etc.

Precision is paramount. Know why things happen, not just that they do. Make every effort to investigate and check the accuracy of the detail.

P5 is Personal Life

For me, the most important aspect of my business life is my personal life! By this, I mean that if I did not have a stable, happy and well-balanced personal life, I know I could not succeed to the same extent in my business life.

The logic here should be quite clear, but many people miss the obvious. Without a balance between the business and personal, life itself becomes tedious and mundane. You cannot give of your best because you get caught in a rut of almost endless work and no play, and you may not even find time to share your successes with anyone.

To be successful you will almost certainly need to work many long hours and burn the midnight oil over many months and years. I can speak from bitter personal experience of how difficult this can be; and of course this is where the support and back-up of a strong personal life can be essential.

I have always discussed my business life in detail with my wife and son. They know most of the high-level activities that I am considering and how I feel about them, and I welcome their contribution in challenging my ideas and assumptions, before I put them into practice at work. This may sound boring, but it is actually quite stimulating as the issues that affect everyone's life – stress, drugs, money, greed – are exactly the problems that must be faced when running a company.

Whatever you do, ensure you do nothing to harm your personal life. It may well be that by damaging your personal life you ultimately ruin your business!

Useful contact details

The Best Payment Practice Group   Tel: 020 7369 9333
Dome House, 48 Artillery Lane,
London E1 7LS
www.payontime.co.uk

Business Link   Tel: 0845 756 7765
www.businessadviceonline.org/businesslink

The Institute of Business Advisers   Tel: 01246 453322
PO Box 188, Chesterfield, S41 9YE
www.iba.org.uk

Federation of Small Businesses   Tel: 020 7592 8100
2 Catherine Place, London SW1E 6HF
www.fsb.org.uk

British Chambers of Commerce   Tel: 020 7565 2000
Manning House, 22 Carlisle Place,
London SW1P 1JA
www.britishchambers.org.uk

Institute of Directors   Tel: 020 7839 1233
116 Pall Mall, London SW1Y 5ED
www.iod.org.uk

British Venture Capital Association   Tel: 020 7240 3846
Essex House, London WC2

Small Business Service   Tel: 020 7215 5363
1 Victoria Street, London SW1H 0ET

Bibliography/Suggested reading

Built to Last (1988) James Collins and Jerry Porras.
Everything is Negotiable! (1982) Gavin Kennedy.
Exploring Corporate Strategy (fifth edition 1999) Gerry Johnson & Kevan Scholes.
The Seven Habits of Highly Effective People (1992) Stephen R. Covey.
Managing to Survive (1993) John Harvey-Jones.
The Innovators Dilemma (1997) Clayton M. Christensen.
Only the Paranoid Survive (1996) Andrew S. Grove.
Information Rules (1999) Carl Shapiro and Hal R. Varian.
Skills with People (1973) Elizabeth Sidney, Margaret Brown and Michael Argyle.
Body Language (1979) Dr. Joseph Braysich.
The Idea of Ideas (1991) Robert W. Galvin.
Tested Advertising Methods (1997) John Caples.